C000076987

EL PATRON: EVERYTHING YOU DIDN'T KNOW ABOUT THE BIGGEST DRUG DEALER IN THE HISTORY OF COLOMBIA

RAUL TACCHUELLA

Copyright © 2020 by John Galeano

All rights reserved. © The total or partial reproduction of this work by any means or procedure is prohibited without the written authorization of the copyright holders.

CONTENTS

INTRODUCTION

I had a son. Many years ago. Today he would be a gray-haired man and he would share wrinkles and experiences with me. But that could not be possible, thanks to my greed and "El Patron".

I lived a good part of my life in one of the most dangerous neighborhoods in Colombia, there my son was born, raised and died. Our relationship was very good, more than father and son, we were like a couple of friends, I think he was the person who loved me the most and I was the one who loved him most.

The commune where the neighborhood is located is in the northeast of the city, we lived in a humble house, the two of us together with my wife. It was a poor house, with leaks, but I remember that moment as one of the best I have lived, beyond poverty there was a happiness that translated into fraternity and genuine love.

For a child who grows up in this type of neighborhood, the streets are his universe, there they play and learn about the world day by day. It was a bright, happy place. At Christmas everything was like a big family, each one attentive to see what "Santa" brought.

I will not lie, things happened, there was crime and murder. For the State the neighborhoods did not exist so the law was imposed by the gang on duty. If you didn't mess with anyone, nothing happened, except for a lost bullet that pierced your chest. The bad thing was that my son began to mess with them, he chose a side, he was starting to be part a gang and they were almost going to "baptize" him by asking him to kill another gang member.

I was a good father, just as I was his friend, I also knew how to put my foot down when appropriate. I found him on time and locked him at home, after beating him with a stick and warning him of the danger he was in if he chose that life.

This looked like it was sinking in, but one Wednesday afternoon the devil knocked on my door, well not the devil himself, one of his demons. He was one of the hit men of "El Patron", he came to announce to me as well as other neighbors of that humble block of weak and rotten houses, that we had benefited from a house that was a few blocks below, a new neighborhood that had the legal name of "El Patron".

That's where my guilt began, as parents we always want to give the best to our loved ones. Not every day they knock on the door to offer you a new house, made of cement, with a roof without leaks and all the services installed. I knew it came from one of the worst drug lord that bore Colombia, but that was not my problem.

Just like the other neighbors, I also accepted, without hesitation. I did it for several reasons: getting my family off where we lived, moving my son away from that criminal gang and getting new opportunities. I saw nothing wrong with accepting the gift.

Who said that people give free things in life?

That house had a price: my son.

A few weeks later I saw "El Patron" for the first time, they knocked on the door of my new house, I opened and one of his men told me that just as "El Patron" had been good to me giving me this beautiful house, now I had to help him, to lend your child "for a few laps" that they had to do. I did not like the idea, but what could I do, I had at the door a man with the face of having killed several, outside, twenty meters away there was a blue Samurai truck and behind was sitting "El Patron", looking at me, seriously, in Silence, reading my body language. At that time in Colombia we all knew what would happen if we challenged this great boss. My only way out was to be obedient. I can swear that my son had a gleam of emotion in his eyes when he crossed the door.

A few weeks later I learned that my boy was one of the hit men of "El Patron".

The whole world knows how the story of the most terrifying man in Colombia ended. After his death that happened a few weeks after my son's, I left that house and Colombia. Now I live in Barcelona, Spain, from where I write these lines that I plan to turn into a book where I will tell many things that have not come to light and others where I tell the true version of what happened.

Although my son became a hitman and walked with "El Patron" from one place to another, he always took a while to come and share with me and there were many stories he told me first hand, conversations with his boss, attacks, bombs, murders, kidnappings

I met his "irons" (guns) he used, he had one that was its favorite, and it was given to him by "El Patron" himself when they succeeded in killing a famous politician who aspired to become president. Although I did not accept it directly, he always left a package of money on the dining room table, at first I looked at it reluctantly, but then looked forward to it.

Here I am going to tell you how "El Patron" recruited hitmen in the various dangerous communes of Colombia, how this man went from being a poor devil to becoming almost a God for hopeless people and how his step was like a whirlwind that changed for good and at the same time for the lives of all who crossed with him.

I will narrate in first person his ascension, his peek where he enjoyed the highest pleasures a man can have in life, even those low that includes traffic with underage girls, until his descent, the mistakes he was making until he was succumbed to the well-known death, where my son died protecting him in one of the coves.

"El Patron" was a nefarious guy for Colombia, he was the only man who declared war on the State, and he created a society where they saw that the only way was to make easy money, no matter who you had to kill.

He created a society where a man said "you don't know who I am" and took out a gun and put three bullets on his chest.

Without any pride I say that my son was part of them and thanks to him I have this story and these experiences, this is the untold story about "El Patron", one of the most dangerous man that Colombia had.

———————

Warning: Real names, places and even some facts were changed with the purpose of protecting the real identities of many people.

1

FROM THE CRADLE TO THE HIRED KILLER

The young who became hired killers in Colombia were recruited as they recruited my son, although that was not the only modus operandi. The chief hitman named Marino, along with his other hitmen, went to the poorest neighborhoods in the city and contacted the gangs. All of them were recruited and were given small jobs that they fulfilled, little by little they were gaining confidence until they achieved the right to a better position or even reach the nearby ring of "El Patron".

Colombia at that time was a country where murders at the hands of hitmen occurred practically every day. For young people with low incomes and low values, the way out to make money was to put themselves in the hands of "El Patron". When they joined, they were welcomed by an entity called "The Office", a band that still has a monopoly on violence in the city for several decades and was founded at the time by "El Patron".

Over the years, after the death of the great boss, she has been able to stay alive and several leaders have passed by, the authorities have tried to bend her and have caught some leaders. But we all know how business moves between the state and the mafias.

When "El Patron" led her this was a hired network and a debt collection house, there came those drug trafficking debts that they didn't pay. "The Office" was born in one of the best known urbanizations in the city. It was a facade, there "El Patron" met to make plans for his work with drug trafficking. His trusted assassins gathered all those gangs that were loose in the city and made them his private army, not enough with that, he gathered young people who were just entering adolescence and wanted to wield a gun and put them to work, took advantage even to the so-called "gamines" who were youngsters who were in the street and already had all that skill that demands to be able to survive.

I can assure you that at that time "El Patron" was the Boss of Bosses. A crime was not committed without him having any relationship, from the most insignificant death to the murders that resonated in the world. "The Office" was key when this bandit decided to declare war on the State and began paying $ 600 to each hitman who killed a policeman.

My son tells me that the day he left home he arrived at the "El Patron" headquarters, he was excited, with a mixture of fear and emotion because he would finally meet the man they talked about so much in Colombia. He took that experience as one of the most exciting of his life. He was then barely 15 years old. He was a fearless, mischievous young man, he wanted to live and he was fed up with my rules and prohibitions of joining the neighborhood gangs.

Through his veins there was a desire to wield a weapon that resonated, he wanted to feel the vibration of the metal in his hand and almost instantly see the bored flesh. He said he felt like God, gave life when he forgave someone and took it away when he pulled the trigger. He and his boss decided who lived or not.

My son arrived and stood in front of "El Patron", willing to know his fate and willing to obey him until death. The problem they had then was the struggle to ban extradition to the United States. The faith and love that took that man made me jealous, I will not deny it, sometimes I think he loved him more than me "Old man, I would die for" El Patron ", I would do anything for him, "he said once, while he showed me his gun.

El Patron was a man with a power that had no limits, his violence seemed never to end. The land of "El Patron" looked like a city of the Sicilian mafia. All thanks to a man who was born in the poorest hills of Colombia. Places where only workers, employees, people who barely dreamed of any small luxury lived. From there came "El Patron" and also many hit men who dream of having a bicycle or some plastic toy, went on to show off luxurious jewels, branded clothes, large cars, all in a striking way, without elegance, seeking to attract attention between the crowd.

In the Colombian mountains, violence was practiced with violence. Clashes between hired assassins, among those my son, traveled fleeing the enemy, facing off, and killing. From this cradle where hitmen who still had the smell of their mothers' boobs came out in their mouths, and drug trafficking was born that reached state officials who merged with criminals to produce a macro-criminality, the largest bosses who sank in Misery to society and they ran rivers of blood throughout the country. It was a time without hope, without innocent sunrises. A blow that marked a before and after.

I was part of that difficult and criminal moment, I was a silent accomplice of everything my son told. I saw how he came to the wealth from which I also benefited.

The price of that money were terrible crimes, war arts, wounded, dead, thousands of victims, of which I also include myself. From the organization of "El Patron", many more crimes came out; organizations and crimes of those who inherited the empire of evil.

2

A BRIEF HISTORY OF EL PATRON
("THE BOSS")

They say that "El Patron" murdered more than 10,000 people, was a drug king who was obsessed with power and had desires for teenage girls. At his zenith of violence he murdered many police and politicians.

When people tell the story of "El Patron" it is easy to imagine him climbing on a horse, with two revolvers in his belt, whipping the villages of women with helpless children. I do not exaggerate or rely on literary licenses to adorn these words, in fact this man loved to disguise himself as Pancho Villa, although his story goes beyond any bandit who had his horse and guns as a friend. Just as "El Patron" committed crimes, he also managed to gain the affection of a good part of the Colombian people.

This man was born on a date near Christmas in 1949, in a town near a large city in Colombia. He was the third of seven brothers, since he was a child he was his mother favorite, which made him pampered.

Although this was not an impediment for him to develop his ingenuity and creativity. From a young age he showed his desire for money and as soon as he won it, he looked for strategies to continue winning it. His first works were renting bicycles and magazines, such as those of The Lone Ranger, El Zorro, El Santo, among others of that time.

When he reached adolescence he teamed up with his cousin Gustavo to work in a tombstone company, for months they traveled looking for mourners to buy tombstones for their recent departed, but soon these two discovered a way to make more money, they stole tombstones from pantheons of rich families and sold it to recyclers.

His beginnings in drug trafficking were in 1992, he was 22 years old and was known in his hometown for his first steps in crime. Already at that point he had created a band that was dedicated to stealing cars and sell smuggled merchandise, which was just the kindergarten for everything "El Patron" was going to do in the coming years.

This man began to act as an intermediary with the drug dealers and those who took it to the United States. He was a ruthless man, if things were not done as he said he killed the daring and continued as if nothing. This cold blood served him to climb in the world of drugs. Soon he began to take money to his house and his mother would say years later in an interview: "He was ambitious, as we all are, he wanted money to have his family well kept, especially to have his parents, his brothers and well also to keep the woman very well taken care of, but never took a penny from anyone"

In the following years "El Patron" along with his cousin learned the trade of drugs under the wing of a man nicknamed "The Godfather", this allowed them to get quick money in exchange for dedicating themselves full time to drugs. They became bodyguards of the great drug convoys that arrived in the city and that was where "El Patron" began to stand out above the other traffickers, in situations of great tension he remained calm and cold. I didn't use cocaine and even my son told me on several occasions that he considered that those who used it were weak at heart.

This personality made him become a "fly" who is the man in front of the caravan and has the facility to bribe the authorities and prevent those who come behind from being in danger.

His employers saw him as a healthy man who did not drink or smoke, so he guided caravans of up to 40 trucks and this generated a lot of money.

Over the years, the revenue of "El Patron" increased to the point that in 1974 he took on the task of taking cocaine shipments to the United States himself, two years later he built his cocaine processing laboratories and in that year his Cartel was born that led until his death. It was such a structure that included the three mayor phases of the drug world, production, transportation and deals.

This was a magnificent time in his life because he led 80% of the traffic of this drug that came to the United States, at 29 he was immensely rich. His historians tell that he had stated that if at 25 he did not have a million dollars he would commit suicide.

Another of his great philosophy was the phrase "silver or lead" or you let yourself be bribed and you took the money that "El Patron" kindly gave you, or took a bullet. At that time, this leader decided on an ambitious goal that he achieved in part: he wanted to be a politician. In this way he was going to look for a veil of legality in what he was doing. For this, "El Patron" sought to win the vote of the people in various ways, either by building more than 100 soccer fields in the most disadvantaged areas, building neighborhoods for the lower classes and helping many, all of this, of course, with drug money.

An example of all the money that "El Patron" spent on cheering citizens, was seen in social works, including the Pacific neighborhood, where he was born and spent part of his childhood, close by the way to that neighborhood where I received that damn house that stole my son.

In one of these events where he inaugurated a field, Virginia Valdez got off a helicopter, a diva at the time that sought to ingratiate himself with those present.

This made him deserve the hatred of other politicians who called him populist. So this was how this man managed to become a congressman at 32. The greatest drug trafficker in Colombia was a politician loved by the people.

It is believed that his fortune amounted to about 25 billion dollars. His income was so great that he didn't know where to spend it. The first thing he did was buy some 7400 acres of land in a town on the outskirts of his city. He invested 62 million dollars in the Neapolitan Treasury and this ended up being almost an emperor's estate.

There was a central house, many amenities, bars, swimming pools, games room, and dining room for seventy people, fridges where there were tons of food, airstrip, hangar, seventy motorcycles, amphibious cars, trucks, aeroboats, a gas station, stables, medical center and much more.

If everything named seems striking, the highlight in this hacienda was the zoo of exotic animals, there were about a thousand imported animals, without any permission, among which a rhinoceros, camels, elk, hippos, elephants, among others.

In these lands there was no lack of big parties full of young women, armed rampant orgies with women who were paid or forced to go.

As this man grew up in the world of drug trafficking, his evil also grew, with his coming to power, Colombia was immersed in a ruthless narcoterrorism against judges, prosecutors, police, military and politicians. Everyone who opposed that drug kingdom was killed, that's where the demand for hitmen was born, it was always necessary to kill more and more people.

"El Patron" had to say only one word for all the hitmen's machinery to act, "Do it". The thugs didn't stop until they saw that dead man in the urn. The anger of the big boss was unleashed when he was expelled from politics thanks to a politician named Rodrigo Bonilla, who proved that he was a drug dealer and that his financing was through drugs. This accusation cost Bonilla his life. Something similar happened to the owner of the newspaper "El Observador", who was murdered in 1986, for making public the murky businesses of "El Patron". Years later this newspaper was attacked with 135 kilos of explosives that damaged much of the building.

From that time I stopped seeing my son as often as before, since he continued to follow the continuous attacks of "El Patron", my boy was involved in each of the murders that happened as well as in the bombs, one of them, the most remembered one that they put in front of the DAS office, the Administrative Department of Security, entity in charge of the antiterrorist work and that persecuted this drug cartel.

On that occasion more than 70 people lost their lives, in addition to 500 injured. The engine of the truck in which the explosives came ended on the 9th floor, next to the DAS chief's office at the time, that same year a plane was shot down because they wanted to eliminate a politician.

At this time, more than ten thousand murders were attributed directly and indirectly. How many of those had my son executed? All these acts set off the alarms of the DEA and it was the beginning of the end.

Miguel Zarza, one of his great enemies and who suffered attacks with immense bombs, said that "El Patron" was a very talented man, of those born unique among millions, he lamented that his genius has used for evil.

Almost fifteen years before his death "El Patron"

wrote his epitaph, because the United States requested that all those criminals who had committed crimes at their borders be extradited. The great boss seeing this immediately unleashed a wave of crimes that caused Colombia not to extradite drug dealers from the country. Sometime later the president then reached an agreement with "El Patron" said he would not extradite anyone if he surrendered and ended up in prison. He accepted but with one condition: he would build his own jail.

Thus was born "The church" site where there was everything but a prison, had luxurious rooms, gym, soccer field, game rooms and even a natural waterfall. "El Patron" did not spent in it all the time, he went in and out at ease, when the media realized it was such a scandal that the government had no choice but to take measures to really lock it up.

This unleashed a persecution that gave no respite and again began a series of murders with more than a hundred hitmen, in turn the government put together a hunting group to catch and kill him. The strategies of the authorities were effective and every day they surrounded him more, they finally had him in the city and only one call was needed to locate him. "El Patron" contacted his son and was immediately located, he was in a middle-class neighborhood of the city, in a chalet. There he was with other hit men who fell, "El Patron" spoke with his son on the phone and confused the noise of the authorities with a neighboring construction. The authorities broke in, the first floor was empty so they kept searching.

When "El Patron" discovered what was happening, he ran along the same path that one of his trusted hitmen followed, turned his gaze and saw one of the policemen, shot him but he threw himself on the floor. Other police officers covering the other area of the house shot him with an R15 and "El Patron" fell next to his hitman. That day they gun down the protagonist of the evil that changed the history of Colombia.

3

"EL PATRON", HIS SEXUAL DESIRES AND THE TRUTH ABOUT THE 49 GIRLS MURDERED

One of the great mysteries of Colombia is the appearance of 49 murdered young women, which they attributed to "El Patron", it was never proven, but I can say based on what my son told me that yes, they killed them for ease dropping. I'm going to tell you this story from the beginning:

"Little girl, behave yourself, do not speak ill or you may get kill," said "El Patron" to a young lady after having sex and while giving two or three puffs to his pot of marijuana, the only vice allowed .

"El Patron" did not exaggerate, if the girl spoke she died. One of his lovers said that he was a kind, serene man, did not talk much and behaved very chivalrous, gave paternal advice and never talked about his problems. This is one of the two survivors of the attack against the 49 young women.

My son told me that once a girl behaved badly, she had a loud mouth and she said imprudence, some even offensive. She felt powerful for having been chosen for a night of sex with the great Colombian boss. My boy did not know for sure what the young woman will have said to "El Patron" in privacy, but when he sent him to take the girl to the house he said "that girls talks too much, it does not suit us, do the job".

On the way, in a detour my son drew a cross of bullets in her chest. She was found days later. Before being killed, she was also tortured, "El Patron" wanted to confirm that she knew nothing about her enemies. Apparently she knew something, because she did not return home and had a ruthless death.

Why did "El Patron" kill those girls?

My son told me that they discovered some of them listening to conversations that they should not, he told me "the day they took all these girls, there was a meeting with several cartels and some heard what they should not, but that's not all, they started talking about it with the others and in a little while what was something private of, ended up in the mouth of all of them, it was time to get rid of them".

Virgin Girls

"EL PATRON" HAD ORGIES WITH HIS GIRLS, THE ONLY requirement he demanded is that they be virgins. He liked to look for girls from 14 to 17 years old. My son and other men dressed well and went to the ghettos to seek and seduce them, when everything was on their way they offered them money to have sexual relations with the great boss.

To convince them they showed them a pack of bills, they were teenagers, and surely had never seen so much money in their life. My son says that "El Patron" said: "when they see the money they will lose their moral compass."

My son was also in charge of looking for some that were not so young, who were over 17 years old, these were taken to a luxurious apartment that was in one of the best areas of the city. In this place they brought models, candidates for queens or aspiring television actresses.

It has always been said that what attracted women was the money and the enigma that "El Patron" had, but also his reputation as a good husband, since despite all this, there was another face of this man, he was a model husband, married to María Valentina Henao nicknamed the Tata, who was according to the capo himself, the love of his life. He was also a loving father, and was a generous lover of Colombian misses famous in that time.

That was a magnet for many women, some of the least important was money. My son repeatedly had to return the money they gave him to offer to women because they simply did not accept it. They wanted "El Patron".

Each one seeks power in their own way.

My son told me proudly, because he always told me about "El Patron" that a girl, returning to her house, told him excited about El Patron: "he is a protective man, he has a man of his word, what he says he fulfills, he generates a lot of confidence" in a way all women dreamed of finding a "Boss" in their lives.

Others were more opportunistic, they knew that "El Patron" was powerful and could connect them to a newscast or get them a role on a television station. Among his lovers, the capo had Virginia Valdez, a famous woman on television and whom he was madly in love with.

For a long time the reason why "El Patron" murdered those 49 young people has been rambled, it was said at the time that the men on the cartel wanted to get information to locate enemies. The other is that it is said that he was minutes from being trapped on a farm and they discovered that there was an informer and since there was no time to identify which one it was, they killed them all.

This is deduced because "It is better to have a dead girlfriend than a resentful witness in exchange for a few million to betray us to the police" this was said by the hitmen, the solution was to fill them with lead.

The third hypothesis is what my son told me, they were killed for listening to what they should have not. As I did not live that in person I cannot give truth to his words, but I can say that there were many events that I met firsthand through my boy's experiences.

"El Patron" said:

"What's up," he said. Let's see if you get me a little girl like that, right? You know where

you have to take her, to A1... no, better
take it to A75

These codes referred to numbered coves that only hitmen knew.

The women chosen by "El Patron" had to be pure, delicate, and small, with long and very beautiful legs. Once he wanted to reach a teenage girl from a volleyball team that the police used as a decoy but that failed flatly.

They usually used girls from poor neighborhoods, young people without trade who were happy with a pack of money, a motorcycle and even a used car. Although the cars were only for those beautiful enough to deserve it.

My son told me with a laugh "All those girls have a price."

The perversion had more nuances, "El Patron" loved seeing a virgin girl lose her purity with an experienced lesbian. Just as my son was looking for women along with other good-looking hitmen, there was also a woman who was looking for girls interested in experiencing lesbian experiences.

They were caressed and kissed by another woman and "El Patron" enjoyed a lot when virgins exploded in multiple orgasms.

In addition to that "El Patron" had sex toys that he carried in a briefcase called "The Road Kit", inside were vibrators and other lesbian toys.

My son enjoyed many of those girls, "El Patron" allowed them to take several women and put together orgies that were worse than the last days of Caligula. For his part "El Patron" decided to go to rooms where he was alone with his lover or lovers, he did not share this sexual intimacy in a group.

The modus operandi to take a young girl from her neighborhood to "El Patron" cove was to make several stops. They took her from one sector to another and there she changed her car and so she passed several "stops" until she reached the final destination, where the capo was waiting for her night of pleasure, they of course went blindfolded.

The pleasures were sometimes one night, but many times it was four or five days, depending on the vibe that "El Patron" had with them.

Among the great myths of the capo was to take girls from poor neighborhoods to rape and dismember them, but this is not entirely true. My son told me that it happened only once, he said "we took a girl from a neighborhood and I don't know what happened to her in the middle of sex to slap" El Patron ", he got angry and sent her to be dismember, but it was only that time, people tend to exaggerate ".

What I can assure you is that "El Patron" was a lover of young girls, he loved lesbian games and was with many beautiful women from Colombia.

My son also had his slice of pleasure. Although of course, that was only in the ephemeral spring of this era of drug trafficking, then things got difficult.

4

THE WORKERS OF "EL PATRON"

Of the many issues that have been addressed from "El Patron" there is one that is not commented on very frequently and it is because it is not very well known: the workers who worked for him.

I remember when the persecution of "El Patron" employers began, all those workers were persecuted and killed, and although my son did not confess it to me for sure he killed some.

What he did tell me was when he had to look for electricians, builders, plumbers and architects to work on his secret works, these professionals received large sums of money for their jobs, but when they were in the last year of persecution of " El Patron " practically all the workers were killed.

The reason?

It's simple: They were the trusted workers of "El Patron" in more than a decade of constructions with very sophisticated hiding places and were the only ones who could take the authorities to those shelters that now served "El Patron" hiding places.

In the difficult moments of the cartel, the men were killed by lieutenants under the order of "El Patron", so the authorities lost an opportunity to find the coves.

The reason that "El Patron" hired professionals to build his houses was because, during the entire time he was committing a crime, no rural or urban house lacked at least one or two shelters to flee or hide from the authorities.

During the persecution process of "El Patron" more than eighty coves were discovered in addition to the prison he built to hide himself and even to put rifles, grenades, and communication radios, uniforms of the police, army and even dynamite.

This cannot be denied "El Patron" knew how to make his constructions, because no element was left out. That is why in the last months of persecution the authorities went with electricians, plumbers and builders to do their job when they arrived at one of the coves. This helped them discover many secrets in each of these properties.

It was shown that the coves had from false doors to fifteen-meter passages that led to bathrooms and rooms, which were only accessed through complex electronic mechanisms.

These shelters, however, were not the only strategy front that "El Patron " used to hide. Many times he used what was called "Finca Caleta", this name was used because it had up to four escape routes.

These places largely guaranteed the personal safety of "El Patron", which is why the Search Block, in charge of hunting him, were certain that the builders were possible informers and therefore had to eliminate them.

There was so much news of high-value murders, magistrates, politicians and bombings that the death of poor workers went unnoticed.

But the coves began to be located from an operation called Cocorná that was deployed on July 1990, when "El Patron" himself along with another drug dealer named Jorge Ochoa, fled to a fence laid by the authorities to find them in La Plata hacienda, in Magdalena Medio.

A couple of months after this attempt capture, the authorities discovered in the cove a couple of secret passages and four escape routes that eventually allowed him to flee from the authorities.

After the authorities hit this cove, it was when "El Patron" began to kill workers. It was best to prevent a toad from speaking. This as I read I do not remember where, they say that the authorities heard him in a flat call. As I recall it was a conversation more or less like this:

«Do you remember the old man who was there on the road? He knew about the cove» said one man.

«Yes, calm down I'll take care of him» replied "El Patron".

After "El Patron" escaped from the jail he built, a couple of months later, the authorities found many of the coves where there were armaments and even where he met with partners.

In one of the many coves, the Moncada brothers, agents of the cartel, were kidnapped and then executed and handed over to a corrupt policeman and later it was a fact that they used to pretend that the drug traffickers had been caught in a police operation.

One of the many coves was equipped with a mechanism connected to a water tap that, when pressed, released a safety plate and opened a door lined in light blue tile. This was located in the shower of the main bathroom, on this site according to investigators "El Patron" kept some partners who then killed.

In the jail made by "El Patron" there was a secret compartment that had a bathroom and a small room of six meters by five in diameter that communicated to the sanitary of the guard through another door made of reinforced concrete and with iron rods.

"El Patron" laughed because for a few months the police bathed in those bathrooms and never realized anything, when the authorities discovered everything was that they noticed that through these passageways you could reach a room with a bathroom and everything. How they discovered everything, was because a man had his gun rushed through a wall and discovered the secret behind him.

Although the coves were not reduced only to escape routes and secret rooms, there were also a small coves like the one behind a painting of the Divine Child of Atocha where weapons and money were hidden. I speak only of the discovered coves, but there are many that were not found.

One of the workers also designed a very large place in the room where my son was, placed under a fridge 80 centimeters deep a cove that served as a bunker, it opened to a space that occupied the closet, a dresser and reached a false concrete door that led to another room of eight square meters.

In the aforementioned jail, many coves of money and weapons were obtained over time, the site was built in such a way that a creative writer could have written a novel full of mysteries with secret passages.

There is a very curious fact, the builder of this prison was a well-known architect who was arrested during the black days of Colombia, but was later released. It is one of the few surviving workers who worked for "El Patron".

For El Patron, any place was ideal for making a cove, hiding places were discovered in furniture, fire-places, swimming pools, ceilings and even on the floor. Many mechanisms were electric or manual but all had their complexity to open them.

"El Patron" gave everyone a name according to the affection he had for them: The Super-secret was in the Middle Magdalena, where a checkpoint was placed in which a police officer was killed; La Rojita was in Girardota; Los Lagos was in El Poblado and thus, every cove, all baptized by "El Patron".

This man was undoubtedly a genius, in Girardota the researchers found a cove that was an architectural work that had an underground tunnel that ended on the other side of a pool, similar to this there were many other coves in several locations in the hometown of "El Patron".

My son had furniture with double drawers that were quite difficult to detect, in them he hid weapons or money. They were so well done that the prosecution returned some without discovering anything.

It was later with time, after more detailed reviews that discovered that there were very well made hiding places.

The passages built by the workers of "El Patron" were great work, consisted of 10 to 20 meters and the journey ended outside the property, which gave him an opportunity to escape.

The reason why the authorities went with specialized workers was because the bathrooms were checked by plumbers, switches and light bulbs were checked by electricians and the structure by construction masters. If the diameter of the house did not match, we went to construction workers to blow up the walls and discover hidden coves to the naked eye.

"El Patron" was not immune to informers, many coves were revealed by informers, shortly before he was killed, the narco had planned to make a cove in the apartment that served as a refuge for Mario Castaño, a man who was killed on March 19 at hands of the authorities.

Surely you had never heard of these coves "El Patron" or if you had heard something you did not know all the effort that the man put to hide it from the authorities.

How many millions of pesos will this drug dealer have invested to hide?

How much genius was wasted on crimes that changed the history of Colombia?

5

NAPOLES

The coves were not the only thing "El Patron" spent, he had so much money that he order to build an incredible house where his family and his beloved daughter Manuela could live.

For "El Patron", it was a paradise on earth.

For the world, the Hacienda Napoles was the place where kidnappings, murders and routes where drug would be distributed were planned.

It is said that "El Patron" earned more than 15 billion dollars during his drug reign, well, official sources say, but in reality it was more than 25 billion, my son tells me.

Much of that money was invested in buildings, houses, cars, farms, coves and of course, the most famous property: The Hacienda Napoles.

It was located in Puerto Triunfo, Antioquia and had an area of 2995 hectares. It had a whole series of eccentric attractions such as the simulation of a Jurassic park, a colosseum, a house, many old cars and several swimming pools.

But the zoo got everyone's attention, it had 200 species of animals, such as hippos, giraffes, zebras, elephants and ostriches.

Napoles was valued at 63 million dollars. The leaders of the cartel when they talked about work met here and it was also a place of rest and pleasure. There were many celebrities at the time, who were not linked to "El Patron", but who sympathized with him.

In the halls where there were there are incredible parties today, before it was scene where the enemies of "El Patron" had been tortured and killed.

Today the Hacienda Napoles is an attraction where people go to see fun and joy, the things that El Patron did. Colombia has always had the peculiarity of taking money from everything, even pain.

I would never step on that place.

The Beginning of Napoles

MY SON HEARD "EL PATRON" TELL HIS WIFE ONCE:

«When I die, all I want is for them to bury me here and plant a ceiba tree on top. Oh, and never come to visit me, because the body is only a vessel that we are given to be here on earth».

As I understand "El Patron" always used to say where he wanted to be buried at death.

He told my son too. Once they were walking through the zoo of the hacienda and said:

«See boy, if I die first than you, do me the favor of reminding my family that I want to be buried there, » he said as he pointed to the place near some trees.

The lord's wish was not fulfilled, his bones become dust in a common cemetery in his city.

But let's see the beginning of Napoles. "El Patron" searched for more than a year a land that had jungle, water and mountains at the same time, in the helicopter of his property he traveled Caucasia, Bolombolo, Santafé de Antioquia and practically all of Antioquia, but did not find a place that met with all these requirements.

One day a notice arrives at his hands that appeared in the newspaper where they offered a farm in Puerto Triunfo, near the Medellín-Bogotá highway. An ideal land for the Hacienda because roads were built near there. "El Patron" agreed to meet the owner and between one thing and another the trip was postponed for three months until it finally happened.

At that time, "El Patron" was with a motorcycle fever and they saw that it would be fun drive in it to meet the owner of the farm. But he was not counting with the rainy season and he got soaked, they still continued despite the ruggedness of the trip and the constant falls.

When night fell they were still halfway through the municipality of San Carlos.

It was one in the morning, but it didn't take them long to find the owners of the store, the restaurant and the hotel. In a short time everything was open and they bought clothes, gave themselves a banquet and went to sleep.

The next day between stumbles and the occasional mishap they finally arrived at the Hazzen Hacienda, there they met the owner who for reasons of destiny was an old enemy of "El Patron", one with whom he had a fight years ago in a neighborhood.

Although the subject was not touched, both men went on horseback to tour the farm and when "El Patron" asked him the price, the owner told him that it was not for sale that was the family's heritage.

The next day "El Patron" went out with his men to tour more farms, saw several and finally talking to the owner, negotiating and releasing some threat between the lines, "El Patron" was made with a property called Valledupar, which he bought for 35 million pesos, which would be more or less 915 thousand dollars of the time.

Although "El Patron" this seemed very little land, so in the coming months he dedicated himself to buying other farms around. In total 9 farms that added more than two million dollars of investment.

Finally I had the desired, a land with rivers, jungle, mountains and a delicious climate with heat but no humidity. My son along with other men and "El Patron" went every weekend to the farm to see the progress of the construction. They expanded one of the houses that would soon be called Napoles in tribute to Capone, the American gangster, whose father was born in the city of Napoles. "El Patron" was passionate of Al

Capone, read how much material came out of the criminal.

Once in an interview they asked him if he thought he was bigger than Al Capone to which "El Patron" replied:

«I don't know how tall Al Capone was, but I think I'm a few inches taller than him».

Soon the main house was erected, it was somewhat strange in architecture but inside it was very comfortable. The room of "El Patron" was strange, it was barely 5 square meters, very small compared to the total area of the house.

On the first floor there were eight rooms about the same size and in the back they had three garages that were for cars, but in the end they put cabins and new bathrooms because the visits were massive.

Next to the pool for children and adults on a semi-covered ceiling was the TV room where 40 people fit; next to this area there was a huge bar with ten tables of four seats, a bar with many bottles of liquor and the site full of electronic games of the time such as Pac-Man, Don King Kong, among others.

One day he took the largest crane in Colombia and used it on the farm to transplant large trees. He planted thousands of fruit trees such as mango, guama, lemon and orange.

One of his great desires was to take the fruits without even getting out of the car.

In that place there was a lot of food, large wineries with tons of food, waiters everywhere willing to offer anything from swimsuits, diapers, shoes, clothes, to many sweets.

Everything was given.

If someone asked for a drink, they gave him the full bottle.

The wife of "El Patron" made tennis tournaments on the court, met with her friends and brought a teacher from the city to train them.

Napoles was fun from start to finish. It was impossible to get bored there.

The eccentricities had no limit, an architect from Magdalena Medio was taken by helicopter by my son, to take charge of building some life-size dinosaurs.

The animals were made of cement and with bright colors. Years later, when "El Patron" fell, some were drilled because authorities believed there was money inside.

Every time there was a meeting in Napoles, the guests were called and asked if they wanted to go by helicopter, private plane, van or motorcycle, they were asked for arrival time and departure time.

"El Patron" was a lover of extreme sports, drove the aeroboats on weekends, sometimes hit the stones and damaged them, but immediately replaced him with another and continued with the fun.

Once when traveling by helicopter, "El Patron" wanted to build a dam using the strength of the Doradal River, for a year he worked on its construction but in the end it was canceled because he was taking a lot of money and lacked technical studies and there was danger to flood several surrounding towns.

The Zoo

ONCE HE WAS AT THE RANCH OF ONE OF HIS CARTEL partners and saw a zoo, he was immediately indulged in building one in Napoles. Interested in bringing animals, he bought a National Geographic library and began to study the climate of the area to select the animals that adapted to that site.

"El Patron" made several trips to the United States, where he bought animals that months later arrived at the farm, his trips were in family and he returned with suitcases full of all kinds of nonsense, bought what he saw, from trinkets to shopping for hours in luxury jewelry stores in the Miami of the eighties.

It was from the golden ages, where no one was chasing "El Patron" and was only enjoying its beginnings in the cartel.

El Patron asked one of his men to find out where he could buy elephants, zebras, dromedaries, giraffes, buffalo, hippos, flamingos, kangaroos, ostriches and other animals. He did not include lions and tigers because "El Patron" wanted the animals to be free and they seemed very dangerous.

Weeks later they gave him information about the animals and then he went to the United States to close the business. It is from there that little-known photo where "El Patron" is mounted on an elephant.

Many animals were not allowed in the country,

because of the issue of fauna, you cannot enter other fauna without authorization or prior studies.

But "El Patron" did what he wanted, so the first batch of animals were brought by sea, but it was somewhat burdensome because it was more than 400 kilometers from the ranch, so the others brought them on clandestine flights that arrived at the small town airports, site where El Patron had two hangars of his property, which facilitated everything.

Also at night, when they turned off the control tower, the lights of a huge landing plane appeared in the sky, a large number of men with trucks left the hangars and in a blink of an eye the animals were unloaded and taken to the ranch.

When the task was over, the plane took flight again and was lost at night.

Everything was fast. When the authorities appeared they got empty wooden boxes and many feathers or fur on the floor.

In this way Napoles was equip with a great zoo.

Once he wanted to have a pair of rhinos and for that he hired an old DC-3 plane that needed to land 1200 meters of runway, but the small airport in Napoles had 300 meters less. The pilot, an old experienced pilot promised to land and he did so, the plane hitting the ground, in its braking process he turned at least ten times but finally slowed down a few centimeters from falling the Doradal River.

The zoo seemed ready but "El Patron" wanted more animals, so it acquired black parrots, he bought them for 400 thousand dollars in Miami. Which by the way made him really upset, because "El Patron" knew from his veterinarian that the animals were neutered.

"El Patron" spent hours in the cage area watching the birds. He had many, but nothing was enough because on a trip he made to Brazil smuggled the blue parrot, with yellow eyes, a protected species, but for El Patron the limits did not exist, one hundred thousand dollars and a trip for her alone in the plane were enough to be in Napoles shortly after.

The last animals to arrive in Napoles were pink dolphins brought from the Amazon and thrown into an artificial lake.

When the zoo had 1200 species, it was ready to open to the public, but something was missing: the entrance. Then a huge white portal was built with the words Napoles in the main columns and a PA 18 Piper single-engine light aircraft above.

The History of the Plane

A LOT HAS BEEN SAID ABOUT THAT PLANE IN THE STORY, but my son told me the real story. This metallic bird says they were the first to carry drug from the bonnet, but the reality is different. It was owned by a friend of "El Patron" and when he landed, it was abandoned at the airport for months, when El Patron saw the pieces he asked his friend to give it to him and sent it to Napoles where they put it together without a motor and mounted it on the columns.

There are also many versions about an old car in Napoles. The most mentioned version was that it belonged to the famous thieves Bonnie and Clyde in 1934 whom "El Patron" admired greatly.

But the reality is also less fantastic, it was the fusion of two cars that were restored and in the end it looked all remodeled and beautiful. This was done by one of the brothers of "El Patron", but one day, the boss arrived in Napoles took out his machine gun and asked his men to shoot it, he wanted to simulate the 167 bullet impacts in Bonnie's car and Clyde.

Although there is a curious anecdote. The shooting almost ended in tragedy because there was a worker inside the car who almost didn't make it.

The hacienda was the beginning of the "El Patron" empire, but just as it was a space for enjoyment it was also a place of terror where drug trafficking activities were organized.

But before that, Napoles was open to the public where the people entered for free. A weekend could be filled with 25 thousand cars. That how popular it was.

He had so many visitors that "El Patron" had to build a road because it was impossible to get there even for him.

Of the animals that brought, only one species could not adapt: the giraffes, which did not get used to, did not eat and in the end they all died.

In addition to the opening, there were constant parties of up to one month in Napoles. They brought famous Venezuelan and Colombian singers, who played all night. There were weekends that the airstrip looked like an airport with so many planes that had been parked.

Regardless of the whole party that was made in this hacienda for "El Patron" his zoo was his baby. Once he saw that the flamingos were not pink and looked almost white. He blamed the food, called an alleged expert who recommended that he be given prawns, but of course, it didn't work.

Another day he saw that the elephants did not eat and as he did not know that he tried everything, chopped grass, sugar cane and even bought three tons of carrots, but nothing. They did not eat.

There in the end he resolved and his animals would eat.

Napoles was so well known throughout the country that they once advertised Naranja Postobon, the Colombian soda company. In the recording they used the Twin Otter light aircraft of "El Patron", amphibious cars, buggies, as well as several animals such as zebras, elephants, giraffes that still lived, ostriches and elk.

The Christmas Gifts

IN HIS SPARE TIME "EL PATRON" NOT ONLY THREW money away, had a great sense of community and helped people. One Christmas my son was delivering toys in all the surrounding areas of Napoles, there was no nearby town without gifts for children.

He gave away good things, toys that you saw on television, no trinkets or low quality toys.

The children received two and up to three toys each.

Once he left the ranch with four helicopters and went to indigenous communities of Chocoan jungles with medicine boxes for those in need. In Puerto Triunfo there were many grateful people, several worked in the ranch and were totally loyal.

Without a doubt, one could live forever in Napoles if we only remember the beautiful moments.

Unfortunately there is more darkness than light.

The Darkness of Napoles

THE CONSTRUCTION OF THE RANCH, IN ADDITION TO being a place of pleasure, was also a place where "El Patron" hoped to have protection in the future.

The first thing he did when he started building the farm was to prepare a space to hide in an emergency. This was in the closet of the main room, put a medium-sized safe where he had money and a gun. It had a cove two meters high and three deep, this space was not visible to the naked eye since it was entered through one of its famous secret and invisible doors.

Napoles had weapons for a war, Colt AR-15 rifles, AUG, guns, Uzbeks, MP-5, even a Thompson machine gun, a 1930s original with a round drum for 300 bullets.

There were so many weapons that next to the pool "El Patron" had an old anti-aircraft battery with a seat, four large legs and cannons with shock absorbers.

Although when they killed Lara Bonilla "El Patron" he expected them to raid the property and had her vanish, she was so well hidden that they never found her again.

In addition to the cove of the main house, there were two others a little far from the ranch, one was called Bakery, a small, modern house, made with large wooden beams and located in the far places of the ranch.

It was a place full of snakes that had to be checked every time they visited.

Another place was called Puppets, austere housing lost in streets with many curves and recesses that would confused you.

In Napoles there were large meetings of the cartel, all the gangsters gathered to do their business. Many went with their girlfriends on duty to show them the ranch of "El Patron".

There my son met the Mexican, a quiet and thoughtful man, who spoke justly. He was a very intelligent man. He also met Carlos Lehder, always dressed in camouflage, olive nightgown and Latin Rambo style, with compass, flares and matches that even lit up when wet.

He was so eccentric that he even carried a crossbow. He had a pair of grenades crossing his chest and a G-3 rifle in his hands.

A crazy guy without a doubt.

This man was armed to the teeth, had an athletic body and a somewhat pale and greenish skin, as if he were sick. Once "El Patron" threw him out of the ranch for being the protagonist of a scandal. That was in 1986, the guy entered the room of one of the men of "El Patron" at dawn and shot him with a rifle. This man commanded one of the hitman gangs.

The reason?

Lehder was furious because the hitman was with a woman he liked.

The scandal and fury of "El Patron" was such that Lehder left the hacienda to never return.

That night the journalist Germán Castro Caycedo was at the hacienda, conversing with "El Patron" when they heard the detonation, el patron ordered everyone to take shelter and went with his men to find out what was happening, at the time Lehder appeared with the rifle in hand and smiling.

«There I killed that son of a bitch».

If it weren't because it would unleash a war inside the cartel, he would have killed Lehder that night.

Napoles, Military Training Center

ANOTHER THING THAT HAPPENED IN NAPOLES WAS THAT it was used as a training center for hitmen. Apart from the other one they had in the heart of the city, here the hitman trained the new recruits.

The reason for the military training has a reason, once "El Patron" said:

«They're very brave here, very cool, but they don't even know how to hold a gun and they get killed like they're nothing».

A large number of "El Patron" men were getting killed, of course, they picked any one, put a gun in their hand and told who to kill. Men with escorts who saw danger gunned down rookie recruits.

Other times they didn't kill them but they had terrible aim, so they had to be trained to know how to shoot, sometimes they would get drunk with a gun.

In 1988, when the war with the Cali Cartel began, I was having breakfast on the ranch, I looked at my son and other men and said:

«These boys have to be trained. There's a foreigner coming who's taught some men of "The Mexican", and I want him to train them. He's from Israel, he's very good. He trained some Colombian military men and is going to teach them protection and security techniques and also teach them how to shoot, to enter commando-style houses, so that these bandits kill each other when they do their attacks or send them to make some runs»

He added:

«We're going to get some stolen cars and an abandoned house to simulate a hostage situation, so they can rehearse. Everyone has to pass, whoever doesn't pass doesn't work for me. Is that clear? »

What he meant by that they will not work for "El Patron" he meant that the one who did not pass should be killed.

A few days after this conversation, the foreigner was brought to Napoles and was taken very early to a farm near the ranch. Yair's was his name. At the time my son didn't even notice it, when he told me I didn't notice it either, not even "El Patron" noticed it, but that Yair was none other than the Israeli mercenary who trained the army of "The Mexican" that would later end up being the group of paramilitaries of Magdalena Medio.

Among the men who trained with "El Patron" high-lighted several, among those my son, along with some of his associates that if I remember correctly were called Tason or Tyson and Tiltan, something like that, I have heard this for years, I turn to the files of my memory.

Those men were lethal. The funny thing is, they came from a family of evangelicals.

During the first few days "El Patron" stood on the side of the runway and watched Yair train his boys, shoot at bottles and cans placed at a reasonable distance.

Many had a terrible aim, they hit the pavement, bullets that were lost on the horizon, resistance train-ing, Napoles looked like a military territory where their soldiers learned survival tactics.

When the training was over, "El Patron" called his boys and asked them about their experiences, they were very pleased with the technique of firing and reloading two guns at once, a difficult maneuver that neither of them knew so far.

Car Bombs

THE CAR BOMBS HAD AS A PLANNING SITE NAPOLES. IT all started when they took a man named Jesus, a man who was an expert in explosives, prepared himself in Cali with a terrorism group from Spain.

One of the Orejuela brothers met him when he was imprisoned in Madrid and brought him, at that time both those of Cali and "El Patron", had no rivalries; the cocaine market in the United States was huge and each had its own area for trafficking.

Jesus became a key man in those times, gave a lot of confidence and "El Patron" gave him a lot of security because he could not lose someone as valuable as him. He became such a reliable man that on one occasion they hid together in a cove.

Jesus learned many techniques for detonating cars with dynamite, such as directing explosive waves to a certain place. The runway of the ranch was available for everything, including for detonation testing.

They stole cars, put the explosives on it and blew it up. The tests were done at the end of the track, near a ravine. On one occasion a car was so loaded with dynamite that it soared through the heavens and embedded itself in a tree at the top of a hill.

When "El Patron" persecution began, he was informed long before the authorities arrived, he had moles in all areas, so when the commission arrived, they took even the last bullet casing.

Every time they raided, the media were proud to say they had discovered guns, drugs and many other things, but there was never anything, "El Patron", my son and the other men took everything.

El Capo was burning with anger when he saw this news.

«There they go, those sons of bitches, slandering me again».

There was everything. Everything happened. Napoles is a symbol of "El Patron".

Another of the great concerns of "El Patron", was the fate of his little animals. he feared they would be attacked by the authorities, he didn't want them moved to other places that weren't fit for them.

He believed that the hacienda was the best place for his animals and that any zoo in the country was horrible compared to the comfort they had in Napoles.

In many of the raids the zoo was left alone, but when things began to get complicated and the chase was cruder, the Institute of Renewable and Non-Renewable Resources took too many zebras from "El Patron".

That's where the real story comes from, when "El Patron" ordered his men to paint donkeys like zebras to replace them.

In order to make the change, he ordered that the watchman be offered payment to look the other way while the men changed the animals.

The watchman in effect allowed the change to be made and that night they painted the donkeys black and white with their stripes. They were donkey-faced zebras.

There was a similar situation when the authorities seized a good number of exotic birds and took them to the Santa Fe Zoo, when he found out he ordered his men to buy ducks, geese and chickens and in the night the men made the change, so their birds returned to Napoles.

6

THE WORST CRIMES OF "EL PATRON"

T here is no doubt that "El Patron" marked a before and after in the history of Colombia. There were many crimes that were committed and I am ashamed to say that my son was coordinator in many of them.

Later I'm going to tell in detail some of them, but first, I want you to have a general picture of all the crimes that happened.

The Number of Attacks

A TOTAL OF 623 ATTACKS LEFT AROUND 402 DEAD AND 1710 injured, all claimed to "El Patron". Many happened at the time of the greatest narco violence in Colombian history. Blood and pain took over the country between 1984 and 1993, when El Patron was shot down.

There were many targeted attacks, bombings in many places, in institutions and media, even blowing up a commercial plane.

My son told me that the murders are not 6000 as the authorities say, but exceed ten thousand. All because of the bombings. There is talk of more than a hundred bombs between September and December 1989, in supermarkets, banks, schools, 85 more between January and May 90 and 10 in December 1992.

These are some of the most remembered attacks for Colombians and for the whole world. And from this old computer where I click the story that marked my life, I remember it in a lot of pain.

Selective Murders

ANYONE WHO STOOD IN THE INTERESTS OF "EL PATRON" was immediately an enemy and became a military target. That's why many political leaders and various personalities who denounced drug crimes were hunted.

Among them and I'm leaving a lot of them out, were:

- Minister Rodrigo Lara Bonilla.
- The director of the newspaper El Espectador, Guillermo Cano.

- The presidential candidate for the New Liberalism, Luis Carlos Galán.

There are many, I name these three because they are the most known, Galán was a candidate of great power, they all said that he was going to be the next president of Colombia, "El Patron" concerned about what was going to happen with his luck if he won, then he killed him in Soacha.

When "El Patron" had the idea to embark on politics, he won a seat in the congress of the republic, the first one that showed to the world that he had ties to drug trafficking, was Lara Bonilla, this cost him the rage of el capo and the prompt persecution to murder him without mercy.

By then Lara Bonilla was Minister of Defense, had been appointed a short time ago. On April 30, 1984, while riding his Mercedes Benz through northern Bogota, two men on motorbikes shot him dead.

The escort chased the hitmen and the driver of the motorbike lost control and crashed into the pavement, died instantly. Later he was identified as Iván Darío Guisado, a member of Los Piscos, a few hitmen from "El Patron" cartel.

His accomplice, who perpetuated the murder was a young man named Byron, was badly wounded but paid 11 years in prison for the crime.

For this crime the then president Belisario Betancur immediately passed the Extradition Act and opened the door to the drug war.

The allegations were harsh from the press releases

of The Spectator, this began to bother "El Patron" who now called themselves "The Extraditable".

By November 17, 1986, there was another crime by the hitmen, it was night when the newspaper's director, Guillermo Cano, was out in his car, and a hitman showed up at the window and shot him eight times with a machine gun. They heard the gunshots in the newspaper, they ran to his aid but soon the journalist died. He was 61 years old, of those 44 he dedicated 44 of those years to the newspaper that was a few months to its 100th anniversary.

The Attorney General's Office declared in 2010 that Cano's crime was a crime against humanity, as it was a systematic and widespread plan of drug dealers against journalism, leaders and political leaders who wanted to end drug trafficking.

A couple of years later, on August 18, 1989, a targeted assassination occurred that would engulf the entire country. After receiving threats and saving himself from an attack, the candidate for Liberalism, Luis Carlos Galán, who was most likely to win, gave a speech in Soacha and was shot from the crowd.

He was taken to Kennedy Hospital in Bogota but died despite medical efforts. The death made an impact on the country. President Virgilio Barco signed a decree authorizing extradition by administrative means, it was no longer necessary to ask the Supreme Court of Justice for permission.

It was at that time that the Search Block was created, a team that brought together police and military forces from Colombia and the United States with about 500 members, with the sole purpose of finding the whereabouts of "El Patron" and his entire group.

Meanwhile "El Patron" kept killing and planting bombs.

Other of the killings were the president of the left-wing party Unió Patrioto, Jaime Pardo, the attorney general, Carlos Mauro Hoyos, the governor of the department of Antioquia, Antonio Roldán, this one by the way was accidentally killed when they were going to kill another, it happened, the hitmen got it wrong and the bomb went off.

Former Justice Minister Enrique Low Murtra, journalists Diana Turbay and Jorge Enrique Pulido were also killed, these murders and thousands more.

Bombs

When the Extradition Act was passed, he began a bloody retaliation against the state. This included the civilian population. Bomb cars exploded every month in many cities across the country.

It was only in 1993, the year when "El Patron" died, and he detonated several cars with explosives. On 30 January in the center of Bogota left 25 dead, on February 15 four more dead in the same sector, on April 15 a bomb went off in an exclusive neighborhood of the capital, this left 11 dead.

There were other attacks in the press, in 1988 a car bomb exploded outside the newspaper El Colombiano, a year later another exploded in El Espectador, three years after the death of Guillermo Cano. In the bomb of the two newspapers there were no deaths, only several wounded.

The Spectator the day after the bombing released a giant headline that read "Let's move on!"

But these bombs are silly compare to the ones that were shocking. They happened in 1989, a year that is considered most serious of terrorism in Colombia.

One of them was the seven tons of dynamite they put on a bus that exploded at the main entrance of the Administrative Department of Security, the well-known DAS. It happened at seven in the morning, 72 were killed and more than 600 wounded. The outburst was heard in much of the city and the shockwave was three blocks wide.

The objective of this bomb was General Miguel Maza Marquez, who was director of the DAS.

In 1991, another car bomb had 150 kilos of dyna-mite and shrapnel, exploded under the bridge of San Juan de Medellín Avenue, just outside the bullring La Macarena. It happened a few minutes after the eighth run of the bullfighting fair ended, many had not left and others enjoyed the surroundings.

The explosion had an expansive wave that threw them away, with blood and dismembered bodies. Tragedy left 26 dead and 134 wounded. This bomb was targeted at an official chariot of F-2 agents of the Metropolitan Police. He was killed, as well as other officers that were there.

Avianca Airplane

THIS EVENT DESERVES A SUBTITLE. IT WAS THE MOST brutal attack on November 27 1989. "El Patron" never took responsibility on this attack, always said it wasn't organized by him, but he did have responsibility.

The story went like this, a commercial plane of the airline Avianca took off from El Dorado International Airport, in Bogota, the destination was the Alfonso Bonilla Aragon International Airport of Palmira, which serves Cali. But five minutes after takeoff it exploded. On board was what they called a "Swiss" i.e. a suicide bomber, he did not know what was in his hands, a bomb that blew up the plane, leaving not a single survivor.

Inside the plane a fire broke out in the central part, from the wings, reached the rear, to one of the tanks and this produced the explosion that completely disintegrated the plane.

In addition to the 107 crew members who died, three people on the ground also died.

The plane's attack was aimed at who was then running for president. César Gaviria. He won the election in 1990, the politician was going to take the flight but for security reasons he gave up at the last minute. Among the dead were three Americans, so the American government was behind the culprits. The only one who pays conviction for this crime is Dandeny Muñoz Mosquera, who pays life in prison in the United States.

7

THE NEGOTIATION ATTEMPTS OF "EL PATRON"

"El Patron" tried several times to negotiate with the Colombian government, when things were getting rough, my son tells me that he was sent to talk to some people in power in order to make a truce with them. "El Patron" said he would turn himself in if they left him his fortune, things were on track, but President Barco repented.

There were several times that he tried, they wanted to negotiate his surrender but although several approaches were made under the table, many people of power were aware of them.

One of the brothers of "El Patron" met several times in a temporary truce, where they attempted a friendly surrender in exchange for the fortune not being touched. Everyone knew this, even America, but the then-President Bush blocked the truce.

As my son tells me, there were many approaches, although this is not allowed by the government, they even erased those documents that were given at that time. The current shame is that these negotiations were advancing after "El Patron" assassinated several presidential candidates, including Galán. Already the blood had run hard in Colombia, but Colombia, as always, lifting its skirts, was moving forward in negotiating with the biggest psychopath in this land of coffee.

This thing I'm talking about here isn't something I'm getting out of the way with the intention of getting a stir up, no. It's born from a reliable source, even from declassified FBI documents and the version my son told me back then.

Here there were many influencing factors, on the one hand was the division within the cartel since "El Patron" was at war with the government.

"El Patron" was willing to dismantle the entire organization, he wanted to leave the drug trade but all this in return for not being extradited, and the only requirement was that the Colombian government allow his family to have his fortune.

In this process even "El Patron" handed over some laboratories and everything seemed to happen successfully, but in 1990 president Bush went to Cartagena and after that the Colombian government backed out.

From there on "El Patron" who until now had shown himself so intelligent and strategist, was now more aggressive, a little weak, and his way of thinking was less rational and more erratic. His action were more like a caged, angry fierce animal.

"El Patron" devoted himself to the war, left the business to others who managed production, shipment and sale. The behavior of "El Patron" was more erratic and this cost him many friendships since those who visited him and knew that he was a drug dealer, now with his double morals did not visit him.

Now "El Patron" had lost control and the circle of friendships had been reduced to a third, as a result of bombs and murders. Already the people of Colombia were tired of the fear, they wanted the war to end. I remember then that Colombians lived in fear, if someone left a box or a suitcase, they were all running, they were afraid, they thought it was a bomb, but in all cases when the bomb squad came they were just forgotten objects.

The health of "El Patron" was affected by all this, my son tells me that in recent times he was nervous all the time, was fatter than he had ever been, he was easily distracted, he was anxious and also suffering a strong gastritis. His health deteriorated, the kind and sociable person, the guy everyone was gone. He was just a madman, even my son was afraid of him.

During his time of persecution although there were versions that he was out of the country, he always remained in Antioquia, where he was much respected.

The fear spread to other colleagues on the cartel, several turned their backs on him, and many of his allies did not support the war against the government so several surrendered to the authorities or said they would leave. Over time "El Patron" made alliances with other weaker groups and some took their operations to other countries.

Everything got complicated when they started having problems with the Cali cartel, there everything went to hell. The Cali cartel negotiated with others among those the Middle Magdalena Self-Defense, the plan was to assassinate "El Patron", and even his head had a price.

The Self-Defense Forces had their eye on him because El Patron put at risk the operations of the Middle Magdalena and had him responsible for many deaths and kidnappings against members of the organization.

The Cali Cartel paid three million dollars for the head of "El Patron."

My son told me that in 89 "El Patron" was preparing a series of strategies to confront the government, all in the face of the hunt that had been unleashed to capture him and send him to the United States.

"El Patron" was furious, because he was going to be sent to prison and the only thing going through his mind was that he wanted to sweep the entire Cali Cartel.

Shortly before the fall of the capo a gang attacked one of his warehouse, this affected a collection of millionaire paintings as well as his old cars.

Another Negotiation Attempt

IN THE PRINT MEDIA OF 1984 THERE WAS TALK OF DRUG trafficking, raids, extradition treaties, hypotheses for the death of Lara Bonilla.

All this happened in the media, at the same time "El

Patron" was at the Marriot Hotel with former President Alfonso López to make a proposal to Belisario Betancur. As the issue progressed, the press found out and the media turned to make a fuss about it and Colombians were outraged.

This happened on May 4 in the afternoon. In a meeting of almost an hour in which López, Santiago Londoño, "El Patron" and José Ochoa participated. The former president was in Panama as an observer in an election. The drug lords were hiding and went by boat to Panama.

They were fleeing for the murder of Lara Bonilla. It was the only time my son visited Panama.

At that time "El Patron" was willing to hand over his routes, laboratories, air fleets and even its distribution connections in the United States. They wanted to surrender to the justice of Colombia in exchange for not being extradited.

He promised that if they took the step they would not send a single gram more and if they did they could extradite them. Lopez took the message to Betancur.

Even if everything was going smoothly for a dialogue, the negotiation was leaked to the press and a scandal was made. The controversy was strong and the House of Nariño, the presidential headquarters, backed down. They published a statement where that meeting Lopez made was behind the back of the government and they did not support her at all.

Many versions have been given of this whole case, the truth my son was not in that meeting, and so I join the many versions. But everything fell down as always because of bureaucracy and mixed opinions.

How many deaths would have been avoided if the words of "El Patron" had been heard earlier? El capo was a criminal, of that there is no doubt, but many of his crimes happened because he was not heard and because of the corruption so great in the Colombian authorities.

But it doesn't matter, history cannot be changed.

8

THE DRUG-POLICY OF "EL PATRON"

Politics was not synonymous with "El Patron" only when he became a senator. There was also a lot of money from the drug trade that fell into the hands of politicians like the then Senator Alvaro Uribe Vélez.

This happened in 1990 where several politicians benefited from El Patron. Several campaigns were funded and several senators won on April 4, 1990, thanks to the money he put in.

The congress that was elected on March 11, 1990 was the first after the death of Luis Carlos Galán, in Antioquia several senators won a seat. All of them belonged to the Liberal Party and the campaigns were assisted by men from "El Patron". At that time the mandate of Virgilio Barco Vargas was coming to an end.

In 1982 "El Patron" won a position as a substitute in the House of Representatives, under the wing of Jairo Ortega Ramírez, with a movement known as Liberal

Alternative that had many ideological affinities with the New Liberalism led by Galán. Seeing that there was something strange about "El Patron", he decided to shake him up and say in the middle of El Patron's hometown that he had no nexus to his ideologies and that he would never support him politically because he was honest.

In '83 El Patron lost his parliamentary immunity.

One of the trusted men of "El Patron" was a representative. He was loyal to "El Patron" because his position had been achieved thanks to the more than ten million funded in the campaign.

That is why on several occasions when operations were being prepared to catch "El Patron" the politician warned and when they came to catch him they only got empty coves.

It's amazing how the story has crossed out the information of the politicians who came to their seat thanks to "El Patron", but many do not count my story, I will not be silent, the corrupt politicians who came to that post thanks to "El Patron" were:

- Alvaro Uribe Vélez, for the democratic sector.
- Armando Estrada Villa, Bernardo Guerra Serna and Dario Londoño Cardona, of the Liberal Directory of Antioquia.
- Federico Estrada Vélez by the sector known as Federiquismo.
- William Jaramillo Gómez, for the Jaramillismo sector.

- There were others who also won at the time, representing various sectors of the Liberal Party:
- Alberto Agudelo Solís, Jaime Henríquez, Gallo and León Arango Paucar, of the Liberal Directory of Antioquia.
- Alberto Díaz Muñoz and Mario Uribe Escobar of the Democratic sector.
- César Augusto Pérez García, Of Liberal Convergence.
- Silvia Mejía Duque del Nuevo Liberalismo, in the Galán sector.

Of the latter I'm not sure if or not he was actually a corrupt.

At the time it was seen that many politicians spent a lot on campaigns, much was talked about, but as whenever you are campaigning the information did not go past a press release or a couple of minutes on a newscast.

There were many hours that were invested in the work of hunting "El Patron" and the information they gathered in the many intercepted calls. Within those calls were the ones they made to the politicians back then.

In these calls "El Patron" always talked to his men, asked for reports, made recommendations, talked about security, called some Antioquians politicians, reminded them of their contributions:

«Remember, I'll help you with money when you ask, Doctor».

Among the many conversations that took place at the time is a memorable one that took place between a senator and "El Patron":

«I need you to appoint someone as deputy director of one of the city's hospitals. You remember the campaign was done with my money. Give this boy the job right away».

«Yes sir, of course. Don't worry he'll be appointed immediately, consider this done. Don't worry».

«Well. I hope for that appointment is done quickly».

The plan was to put Conrado Antonio Prisco, family of one of the gangs of hitmen who committed many crimes under the contract of "El Patron".

Although, this did not play very well, because this doctor was abducted on February 16, 1991 and the body was found lifeless on a street in the municipality of Cocorná, according to what I knew then, at the time of his death he was at the Metropolitan Institute of Health , Metrohealth. Fifteen days after his death he had been promoted to the Diarrheal Disease Training Unit of St. Vincent de Paul Hospital. The death of this doctor was part of the response to the war declared by the Cali Cartel to "El Patron" cartel.

At the time the cartel was fragmented by the raw war. "El Patron" had alliances with other smaller groups and had operations outside Colombia.

At that time "El Patron" met with several politicians in exclusive restaurants. This was a clue to the authorities because they were watching to see what big move was going on in these restaurants to try to catch him.

What the authorities wanted was to see increased activities and recognize food messengers or body-guards, who could be followed to the hideout.

It was necessary this simple strategy to find the many coves of "El Patron" and wipe out the whole cartel that did so much damage to the nation.

It did not matter the work he did with the many campaigns he funded, or the strategies, or the cops he killed, didn't matter at all. Finally the kingpin fell with a rather benevolent death for everything that psychopath did.

9

ECCENTRICITY AND STORIES YOU DIDN'T KNOW ABOUT "EL PATRON"

L oved and hated by many. I hate him, I'll hate him until the last day of my life. My son loved him, loved him to his last breath. The streets of Colombia still love and hate him. They sell T-shirt with his face and people buy them. Entire families mourn for relatives who were shot dead.

"El Patron" is undoubtedly a character in the story. As food for those people who like this topic. Based on what my son told me, I share his life, demystify many of his stories and tell several of his eccentricities.

This is How "El Patron" Was in Intimacy

WE ALL KNOW THAT THIS MAN WAS POWERFUL IN THE world of drugs and in Colombia. It was not for free that the DEA and the Cali Cartel had to get involved in order to get close and kill him.

His life is quite a dichotomy, on the one hand a harsh and cruel man, totally ruthless, led with boundless violence the largest drug cartel in the world. On the other hand you see a family man, who helped people, easily earned the affection of people and many poor people were helped by him.

This man was quite normal in his daily life at home. He was a loving father, he enjoyed his children, played with them. He was therefore the example of a father.

His advice was unique, he often told his son:

«Brave is one who does not try drugs».

Because "El Patron" sold drugs but didn't use them, except marijuana.

He didn't drink alcoholic beverages, he had non-alcoholic beers in his cellar, in the early morning he would sit and think about smoking a joint, but that is it.

One thing this man hated was rude people, he had good manners, he never stopped saying "please" and "thank you," he treated all people with a lot of respect.

In the intimacy he was very pampering with his children, telling stories to his children every night, singing songs by Topo Gigio. In his son's memory the smell that most related to him was beetroot, as he ate much back then several times he felt the smell.

For many years this man was the most wanted in the world, especially by the United States, however, "El Patron" came to the United States like any tourist and took a photo with the White House in the background.

This man came to America and spent too much, gave ten thousand dollars to his sons, and the order was to spend every dollar. Once they arrived at the airport and there were more limousines than people, his son left alone in one watching Tom and Jerry and drinking chocolate milkshake.

The famous photo of "El Patron" with his son and the White House was his favorite, he had it framed in many places, when the authorities arrived he ran out and the first thing that "El Patron" took was that picture, so it was present in many coves and even in the prison he built.

This fact showed, in addition to having his son next to him, the luxury of having taken a picture on the land that sought him, was a feat.

The Decline of Power

WHEN "EL PATRON" FELL DEAD IN DECEMBER 1993, just one day after his 44th birthday, almost everything he had created fell with him. Authorities took Napoles, many animals died, many dinosaurs were drilled, and the decline and abandonment came to many of its properties.

Their hippos did survive, today there are almost 40 specimens that were born from the original hippos. This made them the largest herd outside Africa.

Eccentricities

THESE ARE SOME OF THE ECCENTRICITIES THAT THE circle of "El Patron" had:

DOMESTIC SERVICE

All the women of the domestic service in the Napoles hacienda wore clothes designed for them. They were manicured and pedicured as well as self-makeup courses. All this from the woman of "El Patron" who also received her makeup and hairdressing service daily.

THE FLOWERS OF THE PENTHOUSE

The Monaco building was another of the precious properties of "El Patron", it had a penthouse of 1700 square meters. The flowers decorated the immense property and were taken to Medellin from Bogota in a private plane. They did this every day.

THE NEW YEAR'S HOLIDAYS

Each time the family of "El Patron" celebrated the end of the year in the Napoles hacienda, he ordered the import of immense amounts of gunpowder and fire-works that cost 50 thousand dollars each.

"El Patron" gave half to the men and the other half was for the family. As my son told me, a lot of that stayed in unopened boxes because it wasn't long before it was all used.

Without any pruritus, my son tells me that the "El

Patron" parties were amazing, when they were not the New Year's, they were the ones they did in nightclubs.

Many celebrations were not prepared, but were called suddenly, despite the high risk of such celebrations, there were many elite figures who went among them police and politicians.

Sometimes the party went from a nightclub to one of the ranch, he would board a plane and ended up partying for several days.

The festivities were rare in themselves, they celebrated for anything. At one of those parties they once raffle a Swedish woman who had little time in the country. Everyone participated and one took her, I don't know the fate of that woman.

Of course, at these festivities there was no shortage of liquor, drugs and virgin girls who ended up in monumental where even the most modest ended up wrapped in youthful legs of little girls who were in a place they did not belong.

Many valued the kingpin as the greatest villain of all. Others saw him as a great politician. Not for free, this man wanted to be president.

THIS MAN, THE MONSTER I TALK ABOUT IN THESE PAGES, was someone of flesh and blood, a person who felt, dreamed, and fought. He did good things, although the bad covers up everything he could have done for good.

These are some of the things that this man did and that are not named in the pages that quote him:

HIS FIRST JOB

As a young man he worked with his cousin stealing tombstones in the cemeteries to sell them later. This was temporary because he then went into the business of stealing cars.

VIEW AS A "SUPER HERO"

He devoted himself to social work in the slums, so many people had respect and affection for him. All this is fine, but where it is said that we had to give our children to join his ranks of terror.

This man was called Robin Hood of the people. He kept his word, built soccer fields, painted schools, donated money to hospitals.

HIS LOVE FOR "EL CHAVO DEL 8"

"El Patron" offered millions to the cast of "El chavo del 8" to go to his parties. Carlos Villagrán who played Kiko said he offered a million dollars to each, but that he rejected it, but El Chavo did go.

But my son tells me that they were all there once. They've been treated like kings since they set foot in Colombia. They came and with the greatest of anonymities so as not to cause scandals.

GANGS

My son tells me that every month they spent about $2500 on gangs to collect and store the money.

MONEY

It is said to have once set on fire $2 million for his daughter because she was suffering from hypothermia, he did it to keep her warm.

It was certainly an eccentric life.

10

"EL PATRON" GENIUS AND CRIMINAL

He was a hardworking man, loving husband, loving friend, and even loving with the prostitutes he brought, with the virgin girls, with the models. He treated them all with a lot of love and intimacy.

I told you that this man donated many things, some without expecting anything in return, he just gave it to the people and that's it. He gave money to a lot of sick people that needed for operations. He was also a criminal who killed anyone without any contemplation.

It is complex to understand the mind of "El Patron", but to try to do you have to go to his beginnings, in his early and youthful development.

Her mother, the one who pamper him so much, was a rural teacher and her father a farm manager. He started out in criminal activities stealing vehicles and went into smuggling. But the problem began with his mother who was too permissive and did not clip his wings in time but consented him.

That's throughout his life and even after his death.

Once, when "El Patron" killed cops she was worried about what he was doing, but not so much about the crime itself, but because he was spending a lot of money.

The woman had her darkness there.

Pablo Escobar's Mind was Destroyed from a Young Age

BY THE TIME HE WAS 21, HE HAD A CRIMINAL organization that was composed by his most loyal followers. Then he began to commit crimes and at the same time to help the people in his community.

It was something with two poles, on the one hand helped and on the other destroyed. No doubt this man had a personality disorder. These years I have dedicated to reading psychology books and understanding the various personalities to find the way of acting of this criminal. I can deduce that he fail to adapt to social norms, he was dishonest, a compulsive liar, he used aliases, he scammed others for personal gain.

He was someone irritable, aggressive, had no remorse, mistreating others was indifferent to him. All this marked the bad guy.

The other side?

Someone civic, humanitarian, unconditional with his own, kind, polite, collaborator.

Two different poles without a doubt.

How to Explain these Two Personalities?

ONE EXPLANATION I HAVE DRAWN THESE YEARS IS THAT this man was formed into two realities where there was an immense desire for power and in turn a desire to help those most in need. This characterized him all his life.

There is also the theory that it was only a desire for narcissism and an immense desire for power. That's why some specialists call it a psychopath, one of the characteristics is that of having affective anesthesia, they do not feel guilt.

The emotion that "El Patron" felt was anger, anger or sadness, when things didn't go the way he wanted, so they also label him a moral madman or a madman without delirium. Well, He had his judgment conserved. He could differentiate good and evil but he didn't care about its boundaries, he simply didn't care.

11

THE WAR OF THE DRUG CARTELS

The Cali cartel was a cooperative of twelve or more groups of drug dealers, you could say. Their command hierarchy was stronger than that of "El Patron", they worked more businesslike and tried not to attract the attention of the authorities.

In the late 1980s, Colombia faced fratricidal struggle, "El Patron" and the Cali cartels clashed relentlessly and filled the streets with bombs and terror. Authorities were trying to stop this crime wave and stop drug trafficking to the world's major cities.

In 1989, liberal politician Luis Carlos Galán, favorite in the polls to be president, was assassinated. After that, hundreds of raids were deployed and ten thousand people were arrested, meanwhile from the United States they offered troops, this because of the unease they saw in the power of left-wing guerrillas and right-wing gangs. The two were beginning to ally with the narcos.

"El Patron" in those days warned that ten judges

would die for every extradited to the United States. At the time a US ambassador put more heat when he showed twelve senators and deputies linked to drug trafficking, said that anyone who makes politics, directly or indirectly, has received help from the narcos and many have sat next to some in the Nightclubs.

It was around this time that "El Patron" planted the bomb with tons of dynamite in Bogota blowing up the DAS building leaving an immense number of dead and more than a thousand injured. Many cars destroyed and a 12-story building in ruins.

From 1985 to 1990, the hometown of "El Patron", with 2.2 million inhabitants, had more than 23,000 murders. In 1990, there were 20 daily firearm deaths. Between April and August alone, more than a thousand young people and 300 policemen were killed. Blood was a river that increased its flow every day.

"El Patron" was beginning to lose the battle with the Cali cartel. The latter began to gain ground in international cocaine markets.

The Cali cartel had managed to establish agreements with the Italian Mafia to have routes in Spain, Portugal, the Netherlands, Czechoslovakia and Poland. The DEA estimates that 180 tons of cocaine entered Europe in 1990.

Interpol explained Colombians' interest in sending drugs to Europe: in 1990 a kilo of cocaine cost between 11 and 23 in the United States. It cost between 27 and 35 thousand in Spain and between 41 and 94 thousand dollars in Germany.

Cali cartel took power and a lot of money. Many men around the world in the form of sleeping cells.

This cell thing my son explained it to me once: members of one cell don't know what the members of another do, each has tasks assigned. The cartel sends someone to a place and makes them open a legal business. That person stays there and waits for his mission.

These people are normal, they wake up in the morning, settle in, go out, greet the neighbor, get in the car, go to work, get around the traffic, attend to the legal business, mow the lawn on weekends, make a roast and drink beer with neighboring friends.

Ordinary people who expect to have a pension plan and meet grandchildren.

It's all like this until at some point the business is going to be used to smuggle drugs or laundry money. They are a kind of secret agents, sometimes they spend up to ten years in the organization before they start acting.

Worthy of an American movie, the difference is that it's real.

The Cali cartel did not use planes or boats as "El Patron" did, they were slower at work, using shipments of coffee, chocolates, wood and fruits. The sales structure was carefully controlled, thus preventing capture.

Buyers had to be approved in a lot of detail and had to show a good sum of money beforehand.

"El Patron" was the savage capitalist, with his own army and personality to own the country. The Cali cartel, a modern manager, settles into political power and seeks to operate cautiously with the mafias, without messing with anyone, without doing unnecessary violence.

One Escape and Two Versions

IN MID-1991 COLOMBIAN PRESIDENT CÉSAR GAVIRIA, who won in 1990 and ruled until 1994, said that the war was either won or lost, then he created a special system of faceless judges who protected from threats worked in peace.

He also offered the narcos, a reduced sentence if they surrendered and also promised them that he would not extradite them. All they had to do was turn themselves in, confess to crimes, and return their profit.

In 1991 "El Patron" accepts this offer and surrenders to justice with 14 of his main men, but puts as a condition that he be taken to his personal prison, this was located in Envigado, in his hometown.

The opinion of the time erupts, some believe that it gave in to the whims of the criminals and others take it as a way out to end all the massacre. The United States, for its part, decides to increase the pressure, a Senate investigation denounces the Caribbean island of Antigua, that British and Israeli mercenaries have trained the cartel soldiers. They say this because if you remember at the time there was Yair, the Israeli.

A year later, on July 22, 1992, after paying a million and a half dollars, "El Patron" escapes from his own prison and eludes a fence of police and military. The reason for the escape is because he was been taken to a real prison, because he lived as a king in his own prison house, but the worst of it was that he would come in and out whenever he wanted.

After escaping he gets lost in the jungle along with all his men.

Hypotheses are that the American military wanted to take him to the United States, the other that was a rebellion of the second in command that had been left in charge of the cartel. Regardless of that, the next day the cartel calls Radio Caracol and say:

«The war will now be thorough, against our enemies of Cali and against the senior dignitaries of the government».

Hundreds of motorbikes with hitmen took to the streets to hunt cops. While they killed policemen, "Los Pepes", a group that was born with "El Patron" but were now persecuted, they also did their part and offered high sums for the lieutenants of the "El Patron".

Hundreds killed in 1993.

Ending when they killed "El Patron." He didn't kill himself, he was killed, too fast for my taste.

He got it easy.

One of the toughest moments of Colombia's war was coming to an end. Colombia was now entering a dispersal stage, at least in the hometown of "El Patron".

The Cali cartel, although somewhat affected, kept its operations and structure standing. While the cartels of Cali and Medellin were fighting, other cartels were born: that of the Costa, of Bogotá, of Pereira and Villavicencio.

After Gaviria's tenure, Samper assumed, this one year later he was accused of having received money from the Cali cartel. The issue was complicated when the chief of police in charge of bringing down the Cali cartel, in a motel, was seen in the arms of a woman who was infiltrated into the Mafia group.

Soon after the Cali Cartel fell, although it continued to delinquent and extend its tentacles. Many politicians smeared, many military with dirty hands, a lot of corruption.

It's hard to fight like this.

Even today, 21st century, this continues to happen and will go on who knows how much longer.

CONFESSIONS OF "EL PATRON"

My son was the right-hand man of "El Patron" so they spent together many nights, talking for hours and sharing all kinds of stories. They had forged a kind of friendship or a father-son relationship, even if it pains me to say this, it was happening. My son was talking about the "El Patron" as if he were referring to a father he's proud of.

These meetings served to make "El Patron" confess many stories of his life that never came to light, I share what my old memory still remembers:

«I was twelve years old when one morning I found out that cold blood was running through my veins. It was a Thursday, it looked like any other, but no, that moment changed my life forever. I was leaving school and I saw two men fighting to the death with a machete in hand, the blows came and went unscathed, but one of them slipped and the other took the opportunity to stick the weapon in the jugular.

The blood was gushing out. People hid in horror, they could hear cries in the distance. I didn't run. The blood fascinated me, I stared at the man until he passed away, and the killer left no trace.

There was the metal sheet of the machete, dyed scarlet, I could see it from my innocent eyes. Moments before fleeing, the killer had in his hand the machete, he trembled, at a certain moment our eyes met, he did not take his eyes off me, and it was an eternal moment.

I kept watching him until he escaped.

I went slowly to my house. That was the way I lost my innocence and I was born for the world I had to live in. Not the one that my mother created for me, but the one I saw in the street and deep down in what I faced with many enemies like the rotten authorities who only slander».

This certainly changed "El Patron" forever. Maybe that's when evil was born, only God knows.

My son also told me about the first mission he had to for "El Patron". It was not very exciting, he had to take a girl to a luxurious house built on a mountain by the valley of Aburrá in the east, the modern side of the city, an exclusive site. It was the neighborhood El Poblado, as I ascended I saw the other side of the mountain, the land where I was, where he was born, where my son became a hitman. The toughed school of hitmen in Colombia.

Since it was the first time, the girl would tell my son where to go, he didn't care what she was going to do, my son doesn't know what she was going to do, but when he saw from the rearview mirror he didn't have a hard time guessing. A beautiful and sensual girl, with an eye-catching neckline and a fine fabric blouse. The woman was of fine manners. She was the National Livestock Queen.

For my boy, that woman was like many others who he had taken to bed, although for a while she was kind of her boss because she had to take her and pick her up.

One time, he was ordered to wait for her, he gambled around, sitting, watching life go by, until he saw "El Patron" appeared, approached him, looked at him, recognized who he was and looked him in the eye and told:

«What are you doing here? »

«I'm waiting for Miss XXXX, who went in right now».

He smiled slightly, almost imperceptible, turned around and went into the house without saying anything else.

I'm sure it was funny that he called one of the mafia dolls a lady. The idea is that there was a small connection between the two.

My son for a time had to work as a chauffeur for this girl, he met several coves that he had not yet known since he had not earned the trust of "El Patron". The relationship between that girl and "El Patron" lasted two years, she got out of it an apartment, a car and money.

That is the same time it took my son to become intimate with "El Patron" and become a high-caliber thug. I seems to have written this with pride, but no, I would have preferred a mediocre, failed son to an entrepreneur who dedicated his talent to killing people.

When my son took the job of "El Patron" without hesitation, he began to change his life, simply but without stopping. He did not understand the consequences of his decision, or even that he had just written his death sentence.

On one occasion the girl he was escorting came in a helicopter with "El Patron", this device failed and began to rush to the ground, ended up in a leafy tree while its occupants were driven out into a mudslide.

"El Patron" didn't suffer a scratch, nothing, that is how his life was, a lucky whatever happened not a scratch on him. He was a man with more lives than a cat.

The pilot for his part was badly injured and one of the bodyguards broke his femur, the model had a split arm, luckily for all whenever "El Patron" traveled, there were all his men behind him, they picked up the wounded and took them to a clinic in the city.

The model went several times to see "El Patron", but with a cast, she was less sexy, the relationship was over and immediately my son became close with him.

There began the evil that for years remained and died shortly before "El Patron".

THE DAY "EL PATRON" THREATENED
FIVE ARGENTINIAN REFEREES

There's a little-known story of the day when "El Patron" threatened Argentinian referees with death. He made them see death up close, this was just before the Libertadores final in 1989.

As always, every time foreign referees arrived in Medellin, Octavio Sierra, a Colombian referee, would pick them up at the airport and take them to the hotel.

It was May 1989, the scenery from the airport to the city was beautiful, a clear blue sky and valleys that looked like they were painted in the city of eternal spring. The flowers moved to the rhythm of the wind, happy and colorful. The foothills of the mountain looked like close arms hugging its inhabitants.

Argentinian referees came in a car, contemplating this beauty, proud to have the honor of being part of a match in the semi-finals of the Copa Libertadores de América in 1989.

The game would be led by club Atlético Nacional de Medellin which is one of the greatest of the city and

Danubio Football Club of Montevideo. It was the second game, the first game was tied 0-0 at the Centenario Stadium. Whoever won in this match was going to the final.

«See there, in that place, they hanged a referee, yes, it was a horrible thing ». Said Octavio with a distressed face.

The referees looked at the place, each imagining in their mind what happened.

A little further on, near the downtown center of the city Octavio looks at them again and says with a sad face:

«Right where you're watching, there's the monolith of a referee they killed after an Antioquia game. Sacred face, what a barbarity the madness we live here».

All the referees had pale faces.

Abel Gneco, one of the referees told Octavio:

«Listen to me, don't say who was killed or where, did you hear me? Take us to the hotel and that's it, you got me, kid? Don't say anything else».

This man had gone several times because he was very good, with great conditions. He had often gone to Colombia, especially for the Dimayor which is the Major Division of Colombian Soccer. Although like him there were always other Argentinian referees for high intensity soccer matches.

Finally they arrived at the hotel, already night fall in the city, the game would be the next day. They settled in, accommodated their things, went down for a drink and looked for a place to dine and then went to bed early.

«I recommend that you don't leave the hotel tonight», Octavio advised them.

«Why? » asked Juan Bava, another referee asked.

«You see, people here are partying, there will be no shortage of who drinks too much, there is a lot of euphoria, even tomorrow is a day off, and the public is on the streets I would not want to be insulted or have a bad time».

«Okay» said Carlos Espósito, the center referee. «Then we'll stay at the hotel».

The other men agreed and they all stayed for lunch at the hotel and didn't leave so they wouldn't take any chances.

Before midnight, they all went to rest, had a shared room that was a kind of immense suite.

In the early morning three young men, including my son, with machine guns in hand and with face covered and a man in his 40s, came into the room screaming that it was a police break-in.

«Quiet all. I want you to listen to me. There's 50 grand for each, Atlético Nacional has to win, did you get that? We've come following orders. You have a price here and in Argentina or wherever you go. You have all have a price on your heads, do you understand me? Atlético Nacional has to win which one of you is the referee? » The forty-year-old man said.

«It's me, I'm the referee», Esposito replied by resting his lower back at the head of the bed. At the same time Bava was on the floor, hearing and silently listening.

After hearing the cries of threats, Gnecco appeared

from the other room and tried to calm everything down "Put your guns down, boys, Please, let's all calm down. Tell Skinny, tell the lord who we are." This telling Esposito to speak, he was nervous and did not articulate any words.

In the silence Gnecco looked at the man and said, «Look, sir, we are referees, we didn't come to affect anyone, we're going to play a game with serenity, calm down, put your guns down, please».

The men repeated the threats and left, not before ripping the wires off the phone from the wall and in the hallway shouting «Either Atlético Nacional wins or consider yourselves dead». Gnecco with total courage peered out at the door and shouted «Go calmly... » then from the bottom of the soul came a phrase that came clear to my son's ears:

"Long live Perón!".

Everyone's first reaction when this happened was terrifying:

Esposito:

«Let's get out of this place, get a cab and leave».

Juan Bava:

«Let's make a call and explain everything so they can help us».

Esposito:

«Let's go to the police and file a complaint about attempted bribery».

Juan Bava:

«Call the ambassador or the consul, let's call the embassy».

Gnecco tried to calm them down and sought to make sense of everything:

«Don't worry, let's all calm down. Everything that we do here, these guys are going to know, we're going to play the game, let's not talk to anybody else, let's do all that by the time we get out of here. Everything now is in God's hands, we will do his will. We are decent and are protected by Him».

Juan Bava replied:

«Listen to me well, talking to Esposito, you do what you want, but if in ten minutes the home team doesn't win two goals to zero I will drop my flag, I'll get on the field and I'll score a goal Did you hear me? I have two children to raise»

The next morning they were pick up and taken by car to the Atanasio Girardot stadium, they left them more than a kilometer away and they had to go on foot, under the hot sun. They went into the crowd to be easily identified and threatened at every turn.

When they arrived in the dressing room they saw that there was a garland of flowers on the wall and a crucifix with three candles. One for each if Atletico National didn't win.

Before finishing the first half Atletico National had 3 goals to 0 and in the end they won with a 6-0, goals made from 40 meters, others by unusual defensive errors of a team that was meant to win.

Officially "El Patron" never declared himself a fan of any team, but in private he was an Atletico National supporter. He obviously advocated for this win, this was part of his plan "Medellin without slums" in addition to distinguishing himself above the Cali Cartel.

Although the theory that the other team received a sum of $500,000 to let the other team win is also discussed. This is something that hasn't been proven, even my son didn't know either, because some said yes and other said no.

From what I've seen by now, I don't think it's uncommon that that psychopath paid even God himself to let anyone he wants to win.

«How are you John? » asks Loustau to Bava when they have already returned to their country.

«Want to know something? »

«Tell me».

« I have just been appointed to lead the second match between Atletico National and Olympia in Colombia ».

« Ah, stop, stop, we have to talk. Where are you? ».

The two men met in the cafe next to the AFA and began to talk about how terrible they had it in Colombia with the threats.

Julio Gondrona, when he read the report that was put in the AFA secretariat especially of what happened, asked not to make public. What they put at risk, was his life not the results.

They acted quickly, they made every Executive Committee of the South American Confederation travel to Colombia to witness the last game and that all the members were direct witnesses of the match. This got Atletico Nacional to move its location from Medellín to Bogotá "due to capacity issues". Juan Carlos

Loustau, Francisco Lamolina and Jorge Romero were appointed to lead the match. A luxury worthy of such a difficult final and with many peripheral interests at stake.

Olimpia of Paraguay, had won the first leg in Defensores del Chaco by 2 to 0, went to Cali, the city that competed with "El Patron".

It was argued that they gave logistical support to the Paraguayan club chaired by the great businessman Osvaldo Dominguez, the brothers of the Cali cartel, all of them awaiting that "El Patron" did not give his city the joy of seeing how Atletico Nacional became a winner of the Copa Libertadores.

Loustau, Jorge Romero, Francisco Lamolina and the others stayed at the Tequendama hotel, they were having dinner the night before the big game and a person with a grim gesture, ordinary manners, in black suit, accelerated pace and intimidating gaze stood in front of the table of them and showed a black briefcase while telling them in a low and firm voice:

«Colombia cannot lose more finals », placed the briefcase, touched the bottom of the table while Romero and Lamolina stood up to face the man, he opened the bag and showed the metallic and black gun, ready to be drawn.

But despite all that, Loustau elbowed him, the man struggled, everything look like a problem would arise, but security approached, the man took the briefcase and disappeared quickly, but not before saying:

« Either Atletico Nacional wins or you return in coffins ».

Loustau came from playing the Sub-20 World Cup in Chile in 1987; The Seoul Olympics in 1988, still had ahead the Copa América in Brazil in 1989, the World Cup in Italy in 1990, the Copa América in Chile in 1991, the Club World Cup in 1992 and an Intercontinental final between San Pablo and Barcelona in 1992. He appeared before the Executive Committee of the Confederation constituted in the Tequendama hotel to be able to denounce the fact and say that the conditions were not ideal to play this match. There was a death threat.

After many deliberations and with the collaboration of Lamolina and Jorge Romero, in the end they realized that even under threats they had to play, it was the best option. It was least dangerous route.

Atletico National had to make two goals to go on penalties and three to win the Copa Libertadores. The previous day they had made an attack on the DAS director that cost the lives of seven people.

Two weeks earlier they blew up the studio where the Mundo Vision news was broadcast. All cases were part of the actions of "El Patron".

The terror was alive, the news of the DAS bombing and the Avianca plane with its 109 dead was still hot.

It could have not been otherwise, the referees were impeccable, the match was a two to zero with goals from Fider Miño and Albeiro Palomo and then you had to kick penalties to decide who would be the champion.

The result of the match would depend on penalties?

would the life of the referees with their great tasks also depend on the penalties?

Luis cubilla, who was the manager made the list of his strikers, on the other hand Maturana agreed with his players.

The first penalty was executed by goalkeeper Éver Almeida and went outside, at the end of the third penalty, Atletico National was winning the match by three to two and and so far was champion. Andres Escobar, Palomo Usuriaga and John Jairo Trellez had score.

The fourth shot was missed by Alexis García from Nacional. All this led them to be in a three to three and only one penalty remaining. Loustau and the others sweated and were entrusted to their religious entities.

Olimpia missed incredibly by Gabriel González, Jorge Guasch, Fermín Balbuena and Vidal Sanabria. For Nacional the same happed, Shots by Felipe Pérez, Gildardo Gómez and Luis Carlos Perea were missed.

It was going to the fourth series of one, 17 penalties had been thrown from eleven meters and there was no champion. Loustau looked at the ball, begged for everything to end soon, gave the order to Leonel Álvarez and he scored the winning goal.

Everyone was happy because they had been saved from certain death, on the way to the airport two cars got in the way. Loustau terrified saw thugs with weapons in hand approaching.

« You did not fulfill the agreement. We offered you a briefcase with money and you left it. You didn't get the message ».

He was dragged and transported to an open field about 8 kilometers from the center. He ran fearing to meet a person in the bushes. A friendly person guided him to take a taxi and finally arrived at the Tequendama hotel, they attended him, gave him a hot bath and provided painkillers.

Nowadays it can be said that these referees were saved by little, they understood the message, not that of "El Patron" but that of the meaning of life. They had a second chance.

14

TRANQUILANDIA (TRANQUILITY-LAND), A BIG HIT FOR THE CARTEL

The day that police Special Forces dismantled one of the largest cocaine laboratories in the Medellin cartel, the history of drug trafficking changed.

It was on March 7, 1984, the history of the fight against drug trafficking in Colombia was transformed, that day, a command of Special Forces of the Police and the undercover agents of the DEA dealt a very strong blow to the cartel.

They raided Tranquilandia.

In an area with a lot of jungle located between the departments of Meta and Caquetá it was the place where "El Patron" and his people produced and transported huge amounts of drugs to the international market.

At that time, Police Colonel Jaime Ramírez, head of the operation, was in command. There were 9 laboratories, eight airstrips and 13.8 tons of cocaine totaling 1,200 million dollars. At the end of all this the members of the Public Force destroyed the last trace of that empire that they had built there.

"El Patron" and his people did not wait to retaliate. On April 30 of that same year, when the state celebrated what they did, hitmen led by my son, they murdered Rodrigo Lara Bonilla, Head of the justice department. The man who had begun to cause noise in drug trafficking spheres for reporting crimes committed.

That was the beginning of the cartel's war against the State. All this had not been a problem for the government of Alfonso López that he commanded until 1978 or for Julio César Turbay who ruled until 1982. And then the others began to see drug trafficking as something bad and everything got complicated with the actions of "El Patron".

Maybe that is why in 1982 the power of the main drug cartels achieved its greatest peek. Not in vain, for that time they managed to run a business that allowed them to import currencies that ranged from 800 to 2 billion dollars, that is between 10 and 25% of the country's total exports.

It refer to concentrated income, with the capacity to influence economic life but through small sectors of beneficiaries.

That was the time when the mafias enjoyed the spring of their crimes, Tranquilandia began to break this organization, although by then it was not noticed, but it was the first fissure, then it began cracking, like a house that is at the mercy of the movements of soil and gradually cracks until it collapses.

15

HEROES WHO FELL AT THE HANDS
OF "EL PATRON"

The drug war of "El Patron" not only claimed the lives of the men I have named you here. There are other characters who also fought but are less remembered because there were so many who were public, that they are only remembered by their relatives.

I remember when my son told me that he had ordered Tulio Manuel Castro, a judge, to be kill by order of "El Patron," he was shot in Caracas Avenue on 45th Street, all because he dictated an arrest warrant for El Patron for the murder of Lara Bonilla.

Luis Carlos Galán, Lara Bonilla and Guillermo Cano are the most remembered murders by "El Patron". Where are the other 5,000 murders attributed to "El Patron" and were they forgotten? This includes judges, magistrates, politicians, journalists, police officers who did not accept bribes and reported crimes.

Those who did not accept the phrases "Money or lead" assumed the consequences.

A few years ago they made a television series based on "El Patron", although they were very accurate with the facts, there are many fictional characters, I talk about the Colombian series, not the stupidity that Netflix did where "El Patron" spoke with an Brazilian accent. In Colombia some took it as an apology for the crimes and others saw it as a tribute.

It was inevitable for me not to remember my son's time and not to feel resentment against that man. I felt as if my boy had just die.

The truth is that the series brought out some forgotten heroes with brave actions, people who tried to stop El Patron, but failed.

« He never let his heart be corrupted ».

Said one of the fallen relatives.

It was July 23, 1985 when Judge Tulio Manuel Castro was on his way to meet his wife Aurora to go to the funeral of an uncle. He had called "El Patron" to court. He left in a taxi from his office to Paloquemao, when he got off on Caracas Avenue, some men were waiting for him.

His wife went to his house to wait for him, since he never arrived at the funeral home she went home to wait for him there. It was 11 o'clock at night when she was called to notify her of the attack. She went out to find him and only found a crime.

For her, her husband had never been corrupted, because several times they tried in a good and bad way to force him to accept money. His integrity remains the pride of his family. Born in Boyacá, a student at the

School of Tunja and a school teacher, just like his wife, until he graduated from Law school.

From there he began a brilliant career in the Judicial Branch, was a judge in different parts of Colombia and an assistant magistrate in the Bogotá court. When the minister was assigned the case, he was the first superior judge in the capital. He was appointed magistrate in the Court of Santa Rosa de Viterbo and was going to take possession but he was murdered 8 days before the investiture.

Aurora had to take care of 5 children. The oldest was 15 and the youngest 4. In a newspaper a news came out saying that she had received an apartment from the government, but it was a lie, they never gave her anything.

The wife wanted to investigate and hired an investigator, but little could be obtained.

Another victim said at the time:

« I'd rather die than give in »

He was a very affectionate man, he did his duty, he was an exemplary father. Carmelita Valencia, her widow remembers him with much love. The victim was Gustavo Zuluaga Serna, a magistrate who also wanted to stop "El Patron" and his cousin. The accusation was the murder of two DAS agents who discovered in 1976 a cargo of cocaine hidden in truck tires.

Zuluaga was a very strict man at home, but more than that, he was a loving father who liked to play board games and have a sporadic drink, a man who wanted a girl who could not enjoy. "El Patron" had threatened him several times to drop those charges against him, but he ignored him, was killed and his daughter was born a few months after that.

For four years he had received several phone calls and even funeral wreaths, he lived a hell at home but he had faith that justice would prevail.

On one occasion Carmelita was in her car and the police stopped her, but in reality they were not officers but men of "El Patron". My son told me with laughter that they pushed the poor woman's car and threw it down a ravine. They told her that she had to tell her husband that he had to drop the charges or bear the consequences.

Where my son was speechless laughing was when they told the woman:

« Next time we won't let you get off ».

After that they considered leaving the country, but did not want to leave the family. The daughter, named Angela, did not meet her father, but receives the reliable portrait of her family.

This was a man with a lot of character, very stubborn doing what he thought was right, he preferred to die than to give in, so he was going to issue a fair verdict.

This was a man of great principle that no one broke. But it doesn't matter how honorable he was. "El Patron" had no qualms about sending him to his death.

« MY FATHER WAS A SUPERHERO »

Colonel Jaime Ramírez learned that "El Patron"

wanted to kill him. From that moment he made sure to investigate the smallest detail. He managed to get a motorcycle and an old Renault 18 escort him, even if it was a car that stranded every so often. This man managed to convince the United States government to give him the 300 thousand pesos charged by an informant infiltrated in the Medellin cartel.

Ramírez lowered his guard when this informant told him that the man hired for the mission had appeared dead in the capital of the city. Everything seemed to show that the plan was frustrated, so he left Bogotá for a few days, with his wife and his 16 and 14 year old children.

«We were tired of so much anxiety and being armed all the time »one of his men remembers, that is why they went without an escort to an uncle's estate in Sasaima. It was Monday, November 17, 1986, it was a pleasant day and they felt like a normal family again. But when they returned, it all started, the shots began to rain.

At the entrance of Bogotá a group of hitmen ambushed them and the colonel finished with 40 shots in the body, while his wife received one in the knee, the oldest son one in each leg and the youngest one in the hand.

When they were in the hospital, the three promised something they still hold: not to seek revenge. The best step was to overcome a bad experience as good people. Although the widow lost half her sight, she lived to take care of her children, but was destroyed inside.

For more than five years the family fought for the

police to grant Ramirez a posthumous ascent to general, the rank he was preparing for shortly before he died. He had enough merits, was head of the anti-narcotics unit, was the one that dismantled Tranquilandia, and discovered the plan of "El Patron" to assassinate Lara.

His children say they saw his father as a superhero, he didn't care about money, but doing the right thing.

But after the death of this man the authorities did not even recognize that Ramírez perished in action and its authors went unpunished for this this crime.

This is the disappointment of my country, so many crimes that remained unsolved, without paying culprits, without justice.

THIS IS ANOTHER CASE:

« His hand did not shaking before anyone »

"El Patron" was arrested once and put in the Medellin jail for the ten kilos of cocaine he was carrying and discovered by DAS men in Itagui.

At that time Mariela Espinosa, was a judge of that municipality, assumed this case and did it as if dealing with any criminal but the threats soon arrived. Constant calls to the house, although the phone number changed many times, a notice appeared in a newspaper where they called her crazy.

That was not all, El Patron ordered that the court be burned so that there was no trace of his file and sent a bomb to the modest Simca who he had bought a few days before.

Although she managed to escape, despite all this she refused to bend before the death hunt they put on her.

« If I have to die for putting someone in jail, no matter how important this person is, then I die ».

That was what she said, she kept her word completely, because she died, although she did not imprison the narco.

She was a very fair woman who had no fear of anyone. She was convinced of the perversion of "El Patron" was great but still did his duty.

The woman could be very brave, but the whole family felt fear. In her house they called him "the guy" when they referred to "El Patron".

The judge tried to take this process to the last possible consequence, but El Patron managed to get the case transferred to Ipiales and with bribes he was free in a short time.

As if that were not enough, "El Patron" killed the agents who stopped the truck full of drugs and on October 31, 1989, assassins murdered Mariela in the presence of her mother as she entered the garage of her house.

The crime remained forgotten in the midst of all this drug manure, when the accusatory criminal system began to function, a few years ago, the first courtroom of the Superior Court of Medellin was baptized with her name. Tribute that took effect and brings to light an honorable woman from our Colombian land.

WHAT DID "EL PATRON" WRITE IN HIS NOTEBOOKS?

One of the things that "El Patron" had was a notebook that he always carried in his shirt pocket, it looked like an intimate diary where he wrote constantly and then reviewed it in great detail. He did not take things lightly and more when it came to cartel men or enemies.

What did he write in those notebooks? It is the question that many have asked themselves. They have drawn many theories about it, but I have the answer, my son told me.

The first thing "El Patron" wrote were the names of the men he was going to kill. That rules out the theory that he managed his finances in those notebooks. He had accountants who took care of those things.

"El Patron" is related to the murder of more than ten thousand people, I think I said it at the beginning. Surely many names were written with the calligraphy of this man in those notebooks.

In those notebooks he wrote the name of his future

victim. The name that was in that notebook was a person who was going to die very soon.

The only people who were noted in that notebook and did not die were former Colombian president Belisario Betancur and one of the men who kidnapped his father, the others all died.

In that notebook, he wrote the name of the person who was going to kill, and the hitman who was going to do it. In those notebooks my son's name must be under a dead person's name.

When one of these men could not complete a mission, he looked for another murderer. He also wrote down how much he had paid for those people's heads, if the goal was difficult then the reward increased.

When one of the men failed, he called them to a coaching session where he gave talks that often worked. Because the hitman in question would find the target and killed him.

"El Patron" compared this hits withwinning the lottery, even paying a little more than what the local lottery jackpot gave.

THE HISTORY OF MONACO

T he attack that happened with the car bomb against the family of "El Patron" marked the beginning of a bloody war against the Cali cartel.

This building, the Monaco, is a fortress that "El Patron" created in Medellín, is closely linked to the narcoterrorism that the city suffered in the eighties and nineties.

More than 600 police officers killed, the thousands of people killed, the Avianca plane that exploded in the air, the DAS bombing, a whole dark chapter of Colombia.

It was built with great care, it was built on a lot of almost 5,000 square meters, in the Santa María de Los Angeles neighborhood, in El Poblado, just in front of the exclusive Club Campestre de Medellín, the city's luxury club.

"El Patron" built Monaco in this area in revenge because those of the Country Club rejected him as a member. He bought the lot and made the building, where he could see the club people from above.

It had bars on the roofs, thus avoiding attacks from above. It had a panic room with a vent where they could get in an emergency, especially if the house was attacked with gases.

It had water tanks in case they had to live locked up for many months. It had a vault with security doors to store money.

The main house was located on the last two floors, there he lived with his family. The penthouse was fortified and that was key in security when the Cali cartel put the bomb that seriously affected the building.

The building suffered a lot of damage, but it did not collapse and the family of "El Patron" left alive, although the daughter of El Patron was affected with an ear problem for the rest of her life.

After the death of "El Patron", the government tried to give several uses to Monaco, even if it was the headquarters of the Technical Investigation Corps of the Medellin Prosecutor's Office, but the attempts failed, according to versions because the maintenance was very high.

For years the ruins of that building were shaving the city, they were without any use, except to be one of the forced stops of the narcotours where part of what this drug dealer lived was narrated.

The building was finally demolish in a controlled manner and they used the space for a memorial of their victims.

They will make a park called Inflection as a reference to the change that took place with drug trafficking and the freest city, a space to honor the lives and memories of the fallen and those who lost so much.

Inflection will be a circuit of sculptures, museums, spaces that will narrate the killings that the "El Patron" cartel committed. Next to that, several will be placed, one in the bullring La Macarena, where a bomb exploded, another in the La Floresta neighborhood, where they killed General Valdemar Quintero, commander of the Medellín police.

A tour to memory, seeking to transform art, looking for a way to change the history of Colombia, unless you begin to see with better eyes and leave behind the great crimes that can no longer be changed.

The government insists that it is a strategy to stop giving narcos myth and counteract the culture of easy money that was created in Colombia in the toughest times of the cartels.

THE HISTORY OF THE TAKING OF THE COURTHOUSE

I t was on November 6, 1985 when the M-19 took the Colombian Courthouse. The shadow of "El Patron" was behind that massacre in a country that showed war wherever it looked.

It was a Wednesday, Colombia would suffer one of the most difficult situations that has happened. At 11 and 40 in the morning, the Iván Marino Ospina Command, of the April 19 Movement, forcibly took the Palace of Justice, where the country's Supreme Court worked. It was located in the heart of Bogotá. One of the three powers of the State was taken by guerrillas, the blood would begin to run for the next 28 hours.

The country was facing difficult times, hostages were seen on television, there were people that escaped from the building with their heads down fearing to be shot.

There were army tanks that went through the doors and walls and were looking for guerrillas, the soldiers came and went with rifles up. The information was practically null for Colombians, they did not know what to think, it was not known what was happening, the episode had more than one hundred dead, including civilians, employees of the Palace of Justice, magistrates, military and guerrillas.

The country was attached to the screens watching what was happening. About 140 kilometers from there was "El Patron" celebrating, this was one of the very few who knew that a massacre was brewing and knew how it was going to end. He also knew what time it would end and he counted that every hour that passed would benefit him in the war he faced with then-president Belisario Betancur.

The name of the operation was not in vain, it was Iván Marino to whom the cartel gave two million dollars to finance the attack. But the guerrilla leader would be executed by the Colombian army in Cali, shortly before the taking of the Supreme Court. "El Patron" not only gave them money, offered shelter and even collaborated with weapons, gave him a truck full of weapons of war.

At this time "El Patron" was a friend of the M-19 since 1981, when he founded the MAS, which stands for Death to Kidnappers, after the kidnapping of Martha Nieves, sister of one of the members of the cartel.

It was the guerrillas who kidnapped the girl. That's when "El Patron" commands a war against them. Now the guerrillas don't want five million dollars but one hundred thousand dollars in Panama.

"El Patron" far from destroying them, decides to make them allies for his convenience, it was an opportunity to get more power. It was the M-19 who took him to Panama after they killed Lara Bonilla, he also introduced them to Gabriel García Márquez, there was a friendship that left him favors, pleasures and obligations.

There were three plans:

The first was to discuss extradition to knock it down with President Belisario Betancur.

The second plan was to burn a series of files that were actually burned.

The third was to hit the government because it was an enemy of "El Patron".

Although it is clear that the relationship between Betancur and "El Patron" was not always bad, they both shared the same hometown, they knew each other and part of the campaign was covered by El Patron, five million dollars to be exact.

This is how the low spheres of power are handled.

But when Betancur was appointed to the Judiciary, for "El Patron" it was a betrayal and Lara Bonilla would become a nightmare for him.

What I have already said happened, they kill Lara Bonilla, they kill Galán, they kill so many others. War is declared to Betancur and the taking of the Palace of Justice is a way to weaken the government. I wanted to give him a fatal blow. That is why he encouraged the idea of M-19m on November 7 they were going to discuss extradition, so the guerrillas had a perfect date to act. That's why he gave him weapons, supported them, helped with logistics and had two million dollars so they could attack.

The M-19 attacked with everything, just them, without members of the cartel operating. The entire cartel knew that as soon as they entered they would fall into a mousetrap where they would leave dead.

The incursion of these men became a complete gain for El Patron. He won with the death of the magistrates. He won with the burning of the files and won with the blow to Belisario. He was the only one who won in all this.

Although "El Patron" at the time told M-19 guerrillas that this attack was a suicide, he recommended that they attack the Senate, which would cause a commotion that would force Betancur to sit down to negotiate.

The president would not have attacked as he did, it was safer that in the Senate he would have acted otherwise. In the Senate was the entire political class of the country, the senators, and the friends of the bench. Anyway, another result that he had.

But despite the advice of "El Patron", the men decided to attack and when they came to realize the mistake it was too late, that building was infiltrated for months. In the cafeteria of the Supreme Court they had one of their own, done all this "El Patron" just had to sit with a pot of marijuana to wait for everything to happen and see everything burn.

That day the greatest drug dealer in the history of Colombia was relaxed, without emotion that altered him although he knew what was going to happen that day. He was aware that looking where he looked at the end, this would give him profits.

He knew that since he deployed the retake, which was quick, everyone was going to die, they had lost. He knew that when they killed inside the palace, they were going to kill the president of the Supreme Court. They were going to kill a large number of magistrates, incumbents and auxiliaries.

That was how it happened, there were nine judges who murdered, during the guerrilla operation. Only four survived the rain of fire that occurred. It is estimated that at the time of the attack there were 500 people between workers and civilians.

Hours after that violent irruption, the president of the Supreme Court called Betancur by phone and he refused to attend. Instead he put Victor Delgado, who was head of the National Police and friend of the magistrate to speak with the highest representative of the Colombian justice.

« Victor, you can't let them kill us here, give the order to stop the firing»

That was the request he made to his friend. That was not the only call, there were others where they begged the media that Betancur had to stop the fire. In one of those calls to the media one of the guerrillas took the phone to talk to the journalist:

«Alfonso Jacquin speaking, second in command of the operation. The president of the republic did not speak with the president of the Court and they will all die. The army entered with their tanks and the shots are fired, when they get here, they will all die».

"El Patron" said it that time:

« If you get inside the court palace, Belisario is going to attack you, because a president doesn't care about the Supreme Court ».

All this was crazy, "El Patron" had won, the records were burned, that would affect the extradition, and the only winner of that day was that man.

The former president on his part a while ago apologized to the country for such a fierce act. That old man still suffers from what he did that day.

At least this man asked for forgiveness, which was not done by "El Patron" who died without the slightest remorse for all the blood he shed in Colombia.

WHO WAS VIRGINIA VALLEJO?

Virginia Vallejo was the first vedette that Colombia had, she was the narco's lover between 1982 and 1989.

Her name emerged in the seventies, began as a commercial model, her famous necklines in cookie advertising are remembered.

She was the image of Ritchie pantyhose and was presenters in several local news, such as TV Events, and 24 Hours.

She is an intelligent woman who made little effort to get her job done, she came to work shortly before going on air. The libretto was learned, at that time they had no telepronter and said it without failures. His prodigious memory allowed him to do the job well.

He graduated from Anglo-Colombian school, Vallejo, as a young man, he learned English and French and was characterized by being well informed in the news of English royalty and what was happening at that time in the environment.

She had the attitude of a haughty and vain woman, sometimes she showed pride, she didn't show up if it wasn't fixed. He had a relationship with the director of Argentine television, David Stivel, a relationship after being married to Fernando Borrero. She was so vain that she slept in separate rooms so they wouldn't see her without makeup.

How She Met Escobar

SHE KNEW HOW TO TAKE ADVANTAGE OF THE BEAUTIFUL body she had then, she was one of the first who starred naked on the cover of a magazine. She appeared in the magazine Aldía. She was the dream woman of many.

She was associated with the most powerful people. She was a close friend of several former presidents. She started her career in the world of performing arts, more for her contacts than for artist skills. She was first in the cinema, with films like Colombia Connection in 1979, a parody about a secret agent who seeks to capture a narco, what irony.

At that time, her boyfriend, Aníbal Turbay Bernal, introduced her to "El Patron".

The relationship emerged shortly. What was between them was not a secret, "El Patron" was looking for her in her office, they talked on the phone, she called him by name, they saw each other in discos, even Vallejo interviewed him in a show she conducted. It was the time when drug trafficking was not attacked as it is today.

«I fell in love with him, I think he loved me at one time. I fell in love with a philanthropist, he was worshiped by the people, and I toured with him many sites of Antioquia. He was an idol, he moved crowds».

She was not only close to "El Patron" but to all the members of the cartel. She always looked beautiful, she was one of those beauties of the last century without surgeries, natural, but although she had a little touch of the operating room. She was also a pioneer of plastic surgeries, but mostly because of vanity than because she will need it. He made his breasts, his nose, he even looked for the Brazilian Ivo Pitanguy. That girl could be very pretty, but her mind was not right, in a moment she began to feel that she felt she was being chased, she looked paranoid. At the same time, problems began to appear between her and El Patron.

That link he had with "El Patron" cost her the job of a presenter and they stopped calling her to go on television. In return, rumors began to spread, like a lover had damaged her face or that she had AIDS.

Years later she would explain that she was perfectly well, she told that when she was visiting a count in Germany who had fallen in love. Although no one ever saw that count, namely if it would not be something to fill her weak emotions.

She appeared on television with a part in a novel called Shadow of your Shadow, in Caracol, but problems appeared soon. It was hard for her to learn the scripts, she was late, and she asked for a change of scenes, she wanted them to be recorded at other times. This caused his character to be disappeared soon. She reached the radio in Todelar. She recorded a gossip segment.

That Virginia so intelligent in the seventies had vanished. I was very lonely, very bad, with a great resentment towards the media. He lived away from the family, even from his mother and brothers, one of those brothers was rubbing that he had been with "El Patron".

She had no children because he did not want to lose her figure, the year in which "El Patron" died she left the radio. Since that day we did not hear from her again. After being a vedette and spoiled of society, now it was only absence. It was known that she led an austere life,

She was seen this century, she is still beautiful, but she has vision problems, you can tell by the way she reads, how she walks, she was a woman who slowly began shutting down until she became a sad and lonely being.

Touching loneliness, well yes, that's what she suffers, she is a woman who is isolated and alone. She has been in a kind of voluntary seclusion with her mother, with whom she finally reunited.

Many of those who worked with her wonder how such a beautiful woman fell in love with "El Patron."

How did someone with her talent and the education of a rich girl, though that by his side, she´d be like Eva Perón or Manuela Sáenz?

I think that the personalities crossed, she was a very

intelligent, shrewd woman, and "El Patron" despite his evil was a strategist genius. Their way of seeing the world captivated them, counting on the good side of the capo, which helped the people. The relationship between them began to break when "El Patron" became increasingly bloodthirsty.

Public opinion says that she was used by powerful people, even some cold-blooded people say that the destiny she got is what she deserved.

She speaks badly of "El Patron", but in my opinion if the relationship was so bad why they lasted 7 years together. She talked about being a bad in bed, forcing her to be together ... criticisms of a wounded woman.

Virginia can already be considered an old woman, out there with a book by Neruda in her hands, there are poems dedicated by "El Patron" and Santofimio Botero. In the pages of the poems desperate Song, Virginia wrote the date of death of her former lover: December 2nd, 1993.

These are verses that she dedicated when she saw that this man died words that he repeated with pain in his loneliness and blindness.

Everything about you was shipwreck.

Now she published a book where she tells everything that happened with El Patron and is also a television presenter, it seems that she finally made peace with karma and can live her last years with a bit of dignity.

20

THE RELATIONSHIP BETWEEN GABRIEL AND "EL PATRON"

Between "El Patron" and Gabriel García Márquez there was no relationship of friendship, this is something little known, of course, nobody wants to know that the most beloved man in Colombia has been related to the worst monster in the country.

My son says that "El Patron" loved to read at night, but he didn't do it frequently, that is, he wasn't a book eater, but he did read some works and in one of his houses he had a library where there were several books from him.

He had great respect for him and called him "The Master."

The book called "News of a kidnapping", one of the most successful of the writer is based on the kidnappings made by Los Extraditables. This book News of kidnapping was published in 1996 and focuses on ten kidnappings devised by "El Patron." That book was built based on the interviews he conducted with the kidnap victims and several politicians of that time.

Gabo was never seen in person with "El Patron." After the murder of Lara Bonilla and the violence in the country by the Cali cartel, it was said that the writer met with El Patron, but this is false unless my son has not learned.

The cartel did have relations with several personalities, including those of Fidel Castro and his brother Raul. Gabo once served as a messenger, one of the men took a thick letter to Mexico and handed it to the Nobel Prize for Literature, the idea was to take it to Fidel Castro. It was a thick envelope containing several papers. My son didn't know what that letter contained because "El Patron" communications were sacred.

El Gabo said at some point:

«A drug more harmful than the so-called heroic was introduced in the national culture: easy money. The idea prospered that the law is the greatest obstacle to happiness, that it is useless to learn to read and write, one lives better and safer as a criminal than as good people ».

This appears in News of a kidnapping, as a powerful synthesis of the effect that caused the kidnapping and all the evil that left the story of "El Patron".

21

HOW WAS THE JAIL CALLED "THE CHURCH"

"El Patron" took 406 days to escape from the jail that he built "The Church" he did it to avoid extradition to the United States.

He escaped on July 22, 1992. This was a luxury prison, set in the mountains of Envigado, 25 minutes by car from the city. It was not a common jail, it had a soccer field, gym, natural waterfalls, large windows with incredible views, expensive pictures on the walls and other luxurious things.

That jail was like his house, "El Patron" controlled everything, he even perpetrated many crimes inside the compound. The soccer fields were an excuse for visits by illustrious people like Higuita, helicopters landed there, in that space they also made a general square to make judgments the partners, Kico Moncada and the Negro Galeano were two victims killed inside the penitentiary center. Double bottom trucks entered the jail where alcohol and drugs arrived. There, many capo visitors hid.

A prison with tremendous views of the Aburrá Valley, the central Andes mountain range next to the Medellín River. He also had weapons, dollhouses for his daughter, power stations with equipment to find people, telephones, fax.

In the cell of "El Patron" many visitors arrived, he lived in an unusual chamber, it was almost a hotel room, a double bed, a light table, television, pictures on the walls, shelves with all kinds of books. Right there they had a waterfall with natural water that they used to be able to bathe, wash clothes and even erase traces of blood on their weapons.

The natural space where "The Church" rests is formed by many narrow steep roads difficult to travel. This area is perfect to prepare a leak and hinder the search work outside the prison. Inside that jail, all the men had means to communicate with the outside. Without forgetting what I said at the beginning, the secret rooms and the coves that were not visible to the naked eye.

One of the phases to escape was to use these channels to sow panic in the city, ordered the installation of bombs in schools, one of the men ordered bombs both in schools and in various parts of the city.

« It's going to rain dynamite on everything ». He said.

There the persecution began that would be the last year of life of "El Patron", where he fled more and more while they were gradually closing on him until they took him to Los Olivos and where he was executed or killed himself, everyone who chooses the version that you like the most.

EL PATRON'S RELATIONSHIP WITH NAZISM

This is something that is poorly documented, "El Patron" allied with Klaus Barbie, the leader of the Gestapo de Lyon in World War II. This Nazi jumped to Latin America in his second part of life.

The butcher ce Lyon and "El Patron" are a couple of characters that crossed and are worthy of an American movie. These two had a relationship in the path of crimes.

The relationship between the two resulted in the opening of new routes through Europe, founded what they called the "General Motors of the drug" and in financing a paramilitary group under Nazi orders.

Contrary to what has been extended, the relationship between these two men did not start in the jungle, at all, these two met in a more relaxed environment, they were on a barbecue given by Roberto Suárez, the cocaine king, the same man who suffered the coup d'etat that prompted the government to the dictator Luis García Meza in 1980.

These two met there, it was on January 8, 1981, they drank a good wine and a ate a good grill at a ranch in Santa Cruz in Bolivia. From then on, a murky relationship began where Barbie offered his colleague contacts with old Europe and small planes to take the coca base to the "El Patron" laboratories. This in turn received money to fight the communism of the time.

How these two ended up collaborating?

The root of this goes to 1976, that was the year in which "El Patron" was arrested for the first time for drug trafficking. This is something that incidentally made him think that every bandit has to spend time in jail to have the school of life.

After being short time in jail "El Patron" expanded its business to Bolivia to earn more money and contact other people, make relations with Nazi military and fugitives, among them the butcher of Lyon, Klaus Barbie.

In his words, by then Barbie and the retinue of mercenaries, handled the coca base trade in the jungles of Bolivia, among other things, protected Roberto Suárez's cargo. This was straight out of a movie, the men of "El Patron" saw forty years old men that still wore their War World uniforms of the great Führer,

"El Patron" before meeting Klaus, contacted Roberto and offered to expand the business in exchange for a good portion of money. He accepted without problem, shortly after the two met at a barbecue that was organized.

From then on, Barbie and his men worked on the transfer of cargos of coca from Suárez. In the early eighties, those responsible for controlling the safety of all work were done on the slopes of Santa Cruz and Beni were "The bride and groom of death", hired by El Rey.

At the same time, Barbie continued to act as an advisor to the King and to "El Patron." This was stated by Roberto Suárez's wife, Ayda Levy.

In the year 81, the Nazi and the Bolivian were travelling often to Medellin to advise him on business. So this man not only gave him security in operations but also provided influence in the dictatorships of Bolivia. It was a contact to expand business and a piece that worked for a while with the cartel.

My son, met the Nazi and my boy who was a gunman with a high dead count, shuddered to meet the cold look of that German. He was a man who stared at you with a self-assurance and a dark inside that shook even the bravest.

I guess he got along with El Patron because they both had the same darkness, for proof you just have to see the eyes of "El Patron" in the hundreds of photos he's in. Evil with evil unite.

THE LAST DAY OF "EL PATRON"

The concern that "El Patron" had for his family made him give away his position.

I met an American federal officer a while ago, he worked in the United States Department of Agriculture. In the middle of a conversation he told me that he was in Colombia at the same time that "El Patron" died.

Not only that, the officer had been assigned by the Department of Agriculture to help Colombian agricultural authorities, he said that in the office where he had worked he could hear the live call just before they killed "El Patron."

The capo had just celebrated his birthday day before that call, he said:

« Wait, I hear some strange movements out there »shortly after it rained a good amount of bullets.

Minutes before there was another call intercepted by the authorities and allowed the location to be traced in a two-story residence that he had bought in Los Olivos, a middle-class neighborhood in Medellín.

The funny thing is that this man was very good eluding the authorities and always was one step ahead. In addition to this owning a wireless phone, he made many calls a day. He moved throughout the city and got into different coves, seeking to confuse the authorities.

The Search Block, which was supported by the DEA, had been trying to intercept the calls for fourteen months. A year ago "El Patron" had escaped from his jail.

For almost a year he managed to escape from the authorities, he had the resources to stay in the shadows. That is why in many villages where he hid or the neighborhoods where people passed, he hid and kept silent, but for security he only went through and kept on going to another cove.

Now the collection of favors for the many urbanizations that he built, the reforestation and lighting works, the construction of courts, even created police barracks in various villages, bought fleets and new patrols.

Everyone owed him a favor.

But everything got complicated for El Patron, because he had on the one hand the monitoring of the authorities and Los Pepes who now received money from the Cali cartel and were chasing him.

In the end, what he was doing was finding a way to get his family out of Colombia, but all the countries that were asked for asylum were categorically denied.

So "El Patron" sent his family to Bogotá where they put themselves in the hands of the police to have protection from Los Pepes, they lived in the luxurious Tequendama residences, that was where he called with more despair and calling again and again neglecting his safety.

That day at 2:35 in the afternoon, after tracking the call, the Search Block sent three trucks that had 17 of the best agents in the organization. They arrived at 2:50 in the afternoon at the site.

"El Patron" had just eaten a plate of spaghetti, was without shoes, lying on the bed, talking on the phone, then heard a noise and asked his bodyguard to look.

When they opened the door they saw the police avalanche, they both ran but the bodyguard opened fire, trying to give "El Patron" time to escape.

He was shot and fell down right there.

"El Patron" on the other hand fled through the back door and climbed to the roof of the house, there he received twelve shots, one of them was behind the left ear and that is where the theory of suicide was born.

All of this has base, because in the times where he fought not to be extradited to the United States, he echoed:

« I prefer a grave in Colombia than a jail in the United States ».

Thousands of people attended his funeral, after death this man is still the most visited in the Monte-sacro cemetery in Medellín.

Has this criminal committed suicide?

When he was young he said that if he didn't have a

million dollars at a certain age, he would commit suicide.

It is not known with certainty what happened. Regardless of what happened, at least this criminal is no longer on this earth.

CONCLUSION

So many years have passed since the death of "El Patron" but he continues to cast his shadow of violence on Colombia.

We Colombians who are abroad, with so much time that has passed we do not feel indignation when we are hear the name of "El Patron". As soon as others know where I am from and even the city where I was born, they know what it is to carry the stigma of drug trafficking beyond Colombia.

I've been in Europe for several years, the same thing always happened when someone knew I was from Medellin, they asked me if I could get drugs, if I knew where there was a camel. It is inevitable that they do mention "El Patron" and ask you if you ever saw him.

The fall of "El Patron" along with that of its partner "El Mexicano" a few years earlier, marked the decline of the Medellin cartel. But that little affected the drug business, which annually produces tons of cocaine that go to various countries of the world and affects thousands and thousands of hectares of tropical forests because of coca crops.

Today there are no big cartels as then, but there are some lords that last for months, there are many organizations that do their job and fill entire ranks. There is the Catatumbo and the Nariño.

This man came to sit in Congress, he was one of the pioneers in the bribery of several senators and politicians, the best known case is that of Alberto Santofimio, convicted of the emblematic crime of "El Patron" that went to kill Galán.

The way he worked was replicated and refined by the Cali cartel and the paracos, as demonstrated by the 8000 processes and the parapolitics.

Moreover, the infiltration of the paracos throughout the State and in the security agencies had a direct relationship with "El Patron", not because of himself, but because one of the great leaders of Los Pepes, achieved a war against the capo, it was enlisted in the deepest of the DAS as seen in the research they have done these years.

These contacts and others from the State caused the paramilitary band to be born in the 1990s, this has left thousands dead, mostly civilians under the flags of the United Self-Defense Forces of Cordoba and Urabá.

Among all these men was the renowned Hugo Aguilar, colonel, who showed dark alliances with all the Black Hand that moved in Colombia.

Aguilar requested the discharge one year after the death of "El Patron". For many years he shone as the man who took down the most dangerous criminal in

Colombian history. This is a recognition that facilitated a path to politics.

In the world of crime, "El Patron" still stands. Diego Murillo, a gunman of the cartel, became independent and consolidated and is what works as "The Office" that I named in the beginning, where a collection office operated. This criminal structure is responsible for many deaths and today is in its fifth generation of capos.

In Medellín there are several criminal gangs that maintain their school of hitmen, to boys who still smell like like milk killing adults and keeping in a country as beautiful as my Colombia as a third world country.

A few years ago Don Berna published a book where he talks about how they killed "El Patron", it explains how together with the police they hunted down El Patron.

According to this version, he says it was Rodolfo Murillo Bejarano, aka Semilla, who killed "El Patron".

How did my son die?

It is not worth naming it. He was another hitman, yes, he was one of the great hitmen of "El Patron", but it is not a matter of pride to highlight what he did, he is not the protagonist of this story, neither am I, it is Colombia, it is to show the story that has been written in many versions but with real data and facts, because I tell it based on what someone who lived it firsthand told me. Even if he is a person of interest because he killed some of the fallen heroes.

Why did I write this story?

I think it was a purging, because of this pain that

has accentuated for a many years. All because of the attention they have given to that Medellín monster.

Colombian series, series on streaming channels, movies with US actors and "El Patron" speaking English.

Books of people who have been close to the capo, the son who leaves anonymity, the woman who appears again, Popeye who comes out of jail and re-enters and is now dying of cancer, lovers who tell their versions of the story.

It's so much, how not to remember my son, I feel like he is alive as a wound that still bleeds. I do not write this book to gain a profit, I write it for me, maybe it will never leave this computer, maybe it will go into oblivion as will I when in a short time my God calls me to his side.

Printed in Great Britain
by Amazon

28302028R00088